Turning Points

Turning Points

25 remarkable Australians and the moments that changed their lives

Edited by
Mary Ryllis Clark

Published by Monash University Publishing
Matheson Library Annexe
40 Exhibition Walk
Monash University
Clayton, Victoria 3800, Australia
publishing.monash.edu

Monash University Publishing: the discussion starts here

© Copyright 2022 Mary Ryllis Clark.
All rights reserved. Apart from any uses permitted by *Australia's Copyright Act 1968*, no part of this book may be reproduced by any process without prior written permission from the copyright owner. Enquiries should be directed to the publisher.

9781922633651 (paperback)
9781922633668 (ePDF)
9781922633675 (epub)

Cover design by Les Thomas
Typesetting by Typography Studio
Cover photograph by Midjourney
Author photograph by Dina Kapaklis

Aboriginal and Torres Strait Islander peoples are advised that this book contains images and names of deceased persons.

Printed in Australia by Ligare Book Printers

 A catalogue record for this book is available from the National Library of Australia

Contents

Foreword by Brenda Niall	xi
Introduction	1
Henry Reynolds	11
Anna Funder	21
Peter Doherty	29
Robyn Davidson	41
Anthony Bartl	49
Fiona Patten	57
Gabrielle 'Didi' Dowling	65
Jack Charles	79
Gillian Triggs	89
Andrew Wilkie	95
Julie Sprigg	103
Inala Cooper	115
Stephanie Alexander	123
Allan Fels	133
Meliesa Judge	141
Jane Rowe	149
Peter Sharp	157
Elena Kats-Chernin	167

CONTENTS

Yuot Ajang Alaak	177
Siobhan Stagg	187
Margaret Leggatt	195
Gia-Yen Luong	203
Richard Cornish	211
Rosalie Martin	219
Elizabeth Chong	229
Contributors	237
Acknowledgements	249
Image Credits	251
Notes	253
About the Editor	257

*For my children, Nico, Margery and Quentin,
and my grandchildren, Ava, Angus, Hanna, Banjo, Christian,
Zöe and Sabastian, and my sister Margaret – with love.*

After nourishment, shelter and companionship,
stories are the thing we need most in the world.
PHILIP PULLMAN

Foreword

Brenda Niall

The idea of life as a journey is embedded in our collective imagination. For some, this looks like a straight line. Others see a fork in the road, another way to reach a destination. This can be a road not taken, wistfully recalled by those who are briefly tempted but decide not to risk the unknown. Others take the risk and find that after all it was the right path, thorny though it may have been.

It's the risktakers whose stories interest Mary Ryllis Clark. In a shrewd and sympathetic series of interviews, she has probed the reasons and impulses that led these men and women to take 'the path least travelled'. The motives disclosed vary as much as the circumstances and the outcomes. Some decisions are almost instinctive, touched off by outrage at a wrong to others that must be redressed. Others, equally altruistic, stem from a slow-growing awareness of need. Then there are the inner-directed conversions that show a sometimes-astonishing way forward for an artist whose life in music, writing or painting means dedication, and risks failure.

Everyone who reads *Turning Points* will find reasons to rejoice and to admire. One thorny path is traced by Andrew Wilkie, whose turning point was the year he spent as a young aide-de-camp to the governor-general in Canberra, meeting distinguished Australians and foreign dignitaries. It changed his view of the world and gave him the courage years later to become a whistleblower who couldn't keep a dutiful silence about the morality of Australia's involvement in the Iraq War. Wilkie's military training meant respect for authority. When authority dictated a war based on alleged 'weapons of mass destruction' in Iraq, Wilkie knew the information was false. He told the truth and suffered consequences that very nearly destroyed his life.

Historian Henry Reynolds is another who couldn't keep silent. For him the turning point was the discovery of the deeply embedded evil of racist injustice in Australian life. Reynolds didn't go looking for a cause; the cause found him. Chance took him to an academic post in Townsville, where he and his wife witnessed two incidents of brutal treatment of Indigenous people, one in a jail, the other on the street. Henry and Margaret Reynolds were shocked: they had never thought that ordinary white Australians could be capable of such callous indifference to human suffering. These incidents changed Reynolds' life. His career as a historian took a new direction. When he took a close and scholarly look at our racial past, he found far more evidence of violence and exploitation than our forebears ever admitted. His published work stirred a hornets' nest of protest. In a matter-of fact account of his journey from appalled observer to eminent historian, Reynolds shows how and why he became a prime mover for Indigenous rights in the *Wik* and *Mabo* cases, as well as a truth-teller about our colonial past.

Gillian Triggs' forthright style has earned her much admiration and some outrage. As president of the Australian Human Rights Commission from 2012 to 2017, she exposed human rights abuses in Australia, such as the treatment of Indigenous youth in custody and the mental trauma of the children of asylum-seekers. Triggs is refreshingly

FOREWORD

direct in discussing the impact she has made: 'Not everybody likes strong, self-confident women [but] when opportunities have come my way I have been happy to take risks.'

The opening words in the story of actor and musician, potter and activist Jack Charles are stunning in their matter-of-fact tone: 'For me, the big epiphany happened the last time I was in jail.' Charles was one of the Stolen Generation. Taken from his Indigenous mother aged four months, sexually abused in a Salvation Army home, he had a long history of drug and alcohol addiction and burglary. His turning point was a program of self-discovery, the 'Marumali journey', that was offered during his twenty-second time in jail. Passing on that hard-won knowledge to other 'lost souls' became his mission, and he became a respected Elder.

There is something to wonder at on every page of this collection. You wonder at the choices made and at the way human willpower, ingenuity and courage combined to change so many lives. There are only twenty-five interviews here but as you read you realise that by action or example each actor in a human drama has shown the way to countless others. Each turning point is a beginning. If there is an ending, it's way past our vision.

Introduction

Mary Ryllis Clark

Three Christmases ago a friend gave me a book called *If I Could Tell You Just One Thing* ... It comprised a series of interviews with about seventy well-known people, such as David Attenborough, Joanna Lumley, Richard Branson and Margaret Atwood. The author, Richard Reed, had asked each the same question: 'Given all that you have experienced, given all that you now know and given all that you have learnt, if you could pass on only one piece of advice, what would it be?'[1]

My reaction was lukewarm. Why, I asked myself, would I want to know what Bill Gates or Ruby Wax thinks is the most important thing in life? But to my surprise I found the responses absorbing – each answer was very different, but every interview was inspiring, informative, entertaining and intriguing.

It so happens around this time I was looking at my overcrowded bookshelves and reluctantly convincing myself that I had to cull some books when I came across my copy of Viktor Frankl's *Man's Search for Meaning*. It took Frankl nine days in 1948 to write his short account of life in the death camps of Nazi Germany. To his astonishment, *Man's Search for Meaning* went on to be translated into twenty-four languages and sell more than twelve million copies. His reaction was, 'If hundreds of thousands of people reach out for a book whose very

TURNING POINTS

title promises to deal with the question of a meaning to life, it must be a question that burns under the fingernails.'

I hadn't read it for many years. Instead of putting it in the box of expendables, I took it over to a chair and started to read it again. I couldn't put it down. I was particularly struck by the idea in its pages that the purpose of life is to live a life of purpose.

The thought began to form in my mind that many people would have a powerful story to tell about a turning point that led to them finding their purpose – their passion. These were people who felt that 'burning under their fingernails'. These were people whose stories I would also love to read. I felt there was the possibility of a book combining the Richard Reed approach – asking people one specific question – with Viktor Frankl's wisdom.

I reflected on the most significant turning points in my own life. There were two. One led to a huge upheaval in my life – though not to finding my purpose. One did lead to me finding my purpose – it set me on my path as a freelance writer.

The first was about tragedy. In my early twenties, I married an Australian in London. I had one son, Nico, in 1970 and then another, Christian, eighteen months later. Christian died unexpectedly at four weeks old. There was an autopsy, but the medics couldn't find anything wrong with him and wrote 'viral pneumonia' on the death certificate. Today they would have written sudden infant death syndrome (SIDS) or cot death. My third son, Paul, was born in 1973. He lived for three months. Another cot death. Crushed, we decided to move to Australia.

This led, unexpectedly, to a job teaching European History at a private school in Melbourne. Not surprisingly, I was very depressed at the time and was struggling to survive emotionally. I wasn't a natural teacher. I found the classroom environment hard going. Some years

2

INTRODUCTION

later, my husband was made redundant and had trouble finding another job. I felt stuck. But one night I had a dream about making choices and knew it meant taking the risk of following my gut. I resigned. This was my second turning point.

Within days, an extraordinary thing happened. My first job after leaving university had been working in a publishing company writing long captions for coffee-table books. I loved it. They were the sort of books that people bought for the illustrations and often read only the captions. I was in my element – even more so when one of my colleagues set up his own publishing company and commissioned me to write *Crown of a Thousand Years* – a history tracing a millennium of British history and a pageant of English kings and queens. I was on a roll until I was thrown off-course by the deaths of my two younger sons. After quitting my teaching job, I had a call from Dr Bill Stent, Director of Economics at the Department of Conservation, Forests and Lands. He was a friend of my father-in-law and had seen *Crown of a Thousand Years*. 'What are you doing at the moment?' he asked me.

'Well ... nothing actually,' I said, surprised to hear from him.

'I wonder if you would come and meet the Director of Forestry,' he said. 'Our minister, Joan Kirner, has an important plan for the management of forests in Victoria. It's being presented to the public in the form of a book-length work called "Victoria's Timber Industry Strategy". Unfortunately, the book is being put together by a committee comprising public servants, politicians, timber industry people and greenies. It's a nightmare without a writer in place and the whole strategy is in danger of being abandoned.' He said he had been at a meeting that morning and left in despair. As he returned to his office, he prayed that the book could be rescued – Bill was a devout Anglican. 'Your name popped into my head,' he said. 'You're the answer to my prayer.'

TURNING POINTS

The next day I went to his office, met the Director of Forestry and was offered the job of rewriting the text, working with a retired forester. It was the beginning of my career as a freelance writer in Australia. Almost everything I have written since – other books, articles, a fortnightly column in *The Age* for a lucky thirteen years – is linked to that conversation with Bill Stent.

I began developing the concept for this book by asking a friend, Margaret Leggatt, founder of the Schizophrenia Fellowship of Victoria, if she would be a guinea pig for me. I was toying with the idea of conducting interviews and writing them up in the interviewee's own words. I had known Margaret for many years: in 1994 she had commissioned me to interview several of her clients with schizophrenia for a book called *Altered Lives*. I knew that in founding the fellowship, Margaret had made a huge difference in the lives of others, but I didn't know what had led to her dramatic involvement in the world of mental health – what was the turning point for her? I recorded Margaret over a couple of sessions using the Voice Memos app on my phone and sent the recordings to my invaluable transcriber.

Margaret explained that she had trained as an occupational therapist and, through her work with families at the Malvern Community Mental Health Centre, found that where a son or daughter had schizophrenia, families were under enormous strain. It was the 1970s and the large mental health hospitals were being shut down. Margaret was conscious that a lot of the people she was involved with at the Malvern clinic would previously have been locked up – possibly for life. In theory, they were now being helped to live in the community, but in reality they were being looked after by their parents. It was an incredible burden for families made far worse by the terrible slur of the time that they – the families – were responsible for causing the illness.

INTRODUCTION

Margaret decided to undertake research into schizophrenia. She started with a master's degree, which became a PhD. It was a crucial turning point. She proved that the link between schizophrenia and early childhood experiences was based on flawed research – blaming the families was misguided. She also knew such families desperately needed support. Her response was to establish the Schizophrenia Fellowship of Victoria and SANE Australia.

Happy with the dry run with Margaret Leggatt, I started to compile a list of people I might interview. My list included people from a range of places, a range of ages, genders, backgrounds, occupations and, of course, a range of very different turning points. Above all I wanted to talk to people who were remarkable – whether or not they were household names.

It was Margaret who told me about Julie Sprigg, the woman who became one of the few physiotherapists working in Ethiopia. Julie treated many patients who had tuberculosis, and saw how physiotherapy could be 'part of a plan to help a family gain economic independence'.

Opera singer Siobhan Stagg's turning point was being asked to sing at an uncle's funeral when she was ten. A distant cousin sent her a note afterwards containing money to take singing lessons at her home in Mildura and a request to be invited when Siobhan sang for the first time at the Sydney Opera House. Siobhan is now an international star based in Berlin.

Speech pathologist Rosalie Martin was Tasmanian of the Year in 2017 in recognition of her work teaching literacy to men and women in jail. She told me she learnt at a very early age what a disadvantage it is to struggle with communication: her older brother has a hearing impairment and was bullied by a teacher for it. This experience lit the flame that fuels her passion to help people with language issues.

TURNING POINTS

Historian Henry Reynolds, deeply shocked by the cruel treatment of Indigenous children when teaching in Townsville, switched his focus from lecturing on English history to researching and writing Indigenous history. His books changed the way Australians view the past. It was Henry who suggested to Eddie Mabo that he had a claim to native title.

Some years ago, I sat next to Robyn Davidson at a long lunch in Melbourne. I was amazed at the number of people who came up to her and said, 'Your book changed my life.' In 1977, Robyn walked nearly 3000 kilometres across the desert between Alice Springs and the west coast of Australia accompanied by four camels and, for much of the way, her dog Diggity. That journey became a book, *Tracks,* and later a film.

Robyn told me, 'The trip changed my life radically. It was a turning point in that it took me from one track onto another – not just the trip itself, but also because of what it generated. I had no intention of writing about the trip. It was very personal, very private. I didn't think anyone would be interested and, in any case, it wasn't anyone else's business. I just wanted to be in the desert, and I knew I had to do something large enough to grow me up, to integrate myself as a person, because I was a pretty lost sort of kid. I did the journey with that in mind.'

I was told about Gia-Yen Luong by a friend who heard her speak at a gathering for Rhodes Scholars. Gia-Yen, whose parents were both boat people from Vietnam, gave up a career in law to become a teacher. She loves her work and is committed to raising the standard of education in state schools in Australia.

Driving home one afternoon, I heard Richard Fidler on the radio talking to a man called Peter Sharp about the major turning point in Peter's life. A soulless insurance claim assessor had told him, 'Peter, we're never going to pay you, so if you can't go back to work, what is

INTRODUCTION

the point in you living?' Peter related how this turning point led him on a search to find a purpose; eventually he became an award-winning photographer. It was a great story, as I found out when I interviewed Peter in Sydney.

On that same trip to Sydney I met with Russian-born composer Elena Kats-Chernin. She was juggling single motherhood and meeting deadlines for commissions when her finely balanced life collapsed. Her middle son, fourteen-year-old Alex, was diagnosed with schizophrenia. 'My son getting so sick was the most important event that changed everything,' said Elena. 'It completely changed me, changed my life, changed my attitude to composing. I decided I didn't want to write this edgy, discordant music anymore. It was better for my son when I wrote something soothing. It was absolutely a turning point.'

Writer Anna Funder spoke to me about giving up her work as a lawyer for full-time writing:

> I am inspired by a mixture of things, but if I look at the books I've written, I've been most fascinated by stories that haven't yet been told. In the case of my first book, *Stasiland* (2003), they were stories of ordinary people who resisted the German Democratic Republic (GDR) regime. Those stories weren't being told at the time, for interesting reasons. In the case of *All That I Am* (2011), it was the very earliest resistance to Hitler that hadn't been written about – and what happened to those brave people faced with British appeasement.
>
> I don't think giving up my job as a lawyer was such a big turning point; I was always going to write. Probably for all creative people it's like that. It's part of your make-up and you must recognise it at some point and just do it. Other work I was

doing felt false somehow – it felt like a deliberate avoidance of an engagement with the world, and with words, that was in my nature. Until I write something, I don't really understand it. I am skating on the surface of a reality which I need to pin down and represent before I can see what it really is.

Indigenous actor Jack Charles told me of his turning point: 'The month-long Marumali Journey of Healing program delivered by Aunty Lorraine Peeters and her daughter Shaan Hamann … was really in-depth work. Marumali changed my life forever … It set me on the path of self-discovery, on the "who the fuck do I think I am" journey.'

Perhaps my favourite interview was with quadriplegic Anthony Bartl. He was struck by a speeding car when he was six years old. His spine broke at C1 – the highest level. He was not expected to live, he said, and his parents were put under enormous pressure to turn his ventilator off. Anthony is now in his thirties and is an inspiration to people living with a disability. He controls his finely tuned wheelchair, his mobile and his laptop with his chin. He plays sport and loves dancing, has been scuba diving on the Great Barrier Reef, has flown in a microlight and has made a documentary film about his trip to South Africa.

Philip Pullman wrote, 'After nourishment, shelter and companionship, stories are the thing we need most in the world.' I agree with him. Hearing other people's stories is a privilege – I was always very much aware of that. The sharing is enriching for both the listener and the speaker. Now I invite you to read the stories that have moved and inspired me.

'I grew up with a strong belief in equality and a refusal to accept deference.'

Henry Reynolds

Breaking the Great Australian Silence

In the mid 1960s, my wife Margaret and I were living in London with our firstborn and I was teaching at a state school in South Hackney. It was very much cockney London. Out of the blue I was offered a job I hadn't applied for – a lectureship at Townsville University College, later James Cook University, in Queensland.

I had been applying for a number of academic jobs in Australia and was having little luck. I wasn't a very good prospect, having only second-class honours and no PhD. Apparently Townsville University College had appointed someone else who had let them down because his wife wouldn't leave Tasmania. Quite by chance I had put in for a job at the University of Queensland in Brisbane and, without knowing, had been on the shortlist. The people in Townsville saw these applications, got my name and sent me a telegram inviting me to an interview at the Commonwealth Universities Foundation in London. I went, and about three days later another telegram arrived offering me the job, with all fares paid back to Australia. And so we, also Tasmanians, ended up in Townsville at a time when it was known for the urbanisation of the Indigenous population and Torres Strait Islanders.

Torres Strait Islanders hadn't been allowed to stay on mainland Australia until their labour was needed to upgrade the railway line from

Townsville to Mount Isa. Hundreds of young men came, then started to bring their families, particularly to Cairns and Townsville. At about the same time, the Queensland government changed the legislation confining Aboriginal peoples to their reserves and missions. People on Palm Island, a reserve fifty-seven kilometres off the coast of Townsville, were basically incarcerated till then. Several thousand people lived there, and some of these families began settling in Townsville.

At the same time, Aboriginal workers were leaving the sheep and cattle stations. One reason was equal pay, another was that Aboriginal stockmen were being replaced by motorbikes and helicopters.[2] So, for the first time in fifty years or more, there was a significant Indigenous community in Townsville. However, they were not well received. There was a lot of violence. Margaret and I saw violence to a degree that we'd never encountered in Tasmania.

I don't remember ever having had a conversation in Tasmania about Indigenous peoples. There was almost no one who identified as Aboriginal in Hobart, where I grew up. We were vaguely aware that there were individuals then referred to as 'half-caste' who lived in the Bass Strait, but I had no knowledge of them and no interest at all. My curiosity about Indigenous history began entirely due to arriving in what was a very foreign place. It was more foreign than cockney London.

My epiphany was a visit to Palm Island shortly after we arrived in Townsville. I went with Jim Keefe, Labor senator for Queensland, so this was a semi-official visit. We were being taken around by the superintendent. The island still had many of the characteristics of the old reserve, with segregated housing and two segregated schools. The girls' dormitory had been pulled down, but the boys' dormitory was still there.

At one point Jim asked about a small, rough concrete building standing on its own on open ground. We were told it was the jail. 'Can we have a look?' he asked.

'Yes, okay,' said the superintendent and unlocked the door.

It was dark inside and smelled of urine. We could make out two doors. One, we were told, led to a cell that was empty. He unlocked the other door. The cell was bare, with a barred window, a dirty mattress against one wall and a bucket over in a corner. Sitting on the mattress were two little girls, one maybe twelve and one about nine. They wore ill-fitting dresses several sizes too large. The older girl had some time before smashed her fist through the window and her hand and arm were bandaged. Blood was seeping through.

The superintendent told them to stand up. They were aghast at these Migloos (whitefellas) who'd come to look at them. Jim asked what these young girls were doing in prison and the superintendent said they swore at the teacher. Now, that was astonishing. It was absolutely astonishing.

I saw many disturbing things in Palm Island on that first visit, but that experience led to my most important epiphany. Having taught children of a similar age in both Tasmania and England, I found the punishment deeply shocking. It totally disrupted my view of what Australia was all about. How could this be? How could you have this? It was really like the Third World was just off the coast of Townsville.

I had grown up in Hobart, which was the convict heartland of Australia. The great majority of people living there had convict ancestry and I grew up with a strong belief in equality and a refusal to accept deference. You could force convicts to be obedient, but you couldn't make them deferential. The way they rebelled was to be anti the whole system of deference, which was and remains part of the English class system. So I felt that's what Australia was all about. I didn't get it from books, I got it from the state-school playground and living in a suburb that was overwhelmingly upper working-class and lower middle-class.

My belief was also strengthened from long conversations with my father, John Reynolds, who was a historian – though first a metallurgist, then a public servant. He was what we call these days an oral historian. He used to talk to everyone and ask them about the past. He was one of the founders of the Tasmanian Historical Research Association and wrote articles and history books, including a biography of former Australian prime minister Edmund Barton.

So that's the Australia I knew, but experiencing the racism in Townsville changed it all. One of the striking things in Townsville was that you did come across archetypal Australian bushman types. They'd often come in from the west and were egalitarian and knocked about with all those Russel Ward characteristics of the 'nomad tribe', but they were also absolutely racist, so that was why race was just so important.[3] Margaret and I had no experience of this. We were thrust into it and just got involved.

Margaret was launched into political activism by an incident that happened one day when she was pushing our toddler in the pram down the main street of Townsville. A black body was thrown out of a pub she was passing, hitting his head on one of the verandah posts. The man lay bleeding right in front of her. To the amusement of the customers, she went straight to the barman – an unthinkable thing for a woman to do then – and asked for help. 'Hey, fellas,' the barman shouted, 'this here sheila wants us to help the n****r.' Margaret then hurried to the post office to call an ambulance. However, they refused to come when they heard the wounded man was Aboriginal, saying that he was probably drunk. She then called the police, who said they'd pick him up.

This was Margaret's epiphany. She started a kindergarten (still functioning today) that was the first preschool for Aboriginal and Islander children in Queensland. We immediately came into contact with people who had problems in society. I did the driving, and we would visit many homes as I picked up the kids for the kindergarten. That's when we met Eddie and Netta Mabo. Their eldest daughter, Gail, was one of the first children in the kindergarten, and we became very involved socially and politically. Eddie and Margaret ran the 1967 referendum campaign.[4]

The curriculum during my first year of teaching Australian history at James Cook University was fairly conventional, based on Gordon Greenwood's *Australia: A Social and Political History* (1955). Inevitably I realised that both in that society and in the lives of my students, some of them mature-aged, race was profoundly important. But there was nothing in that book about Aboriginal peoples – they weren't even an index entry. They simply didn't exist. That was typical of all those general histories produced in the 1960s.

One of the problems was that if you wanted to teach Aboriginal history, where would you start? There was nothing in the library, there was nothing much anywhere. You had to do your own research. I sent my first honours student, Noel Loos, to look at the frontier conflict in the Bowen district because the local newspaper, *The Port Denison Times*, first published in 1864, was still in hard copy. He was reluctant and needed persuading. He wasn't sure whether there was enough in it, but of course once he started, he realised this was just an amazing story. It was an absolute revelation.

So that was where it began. Having started with Queensland, and because I wasn't doing a PhD, I could then go all over Australia, which I did for ten years. I researched every library, every archive, all the government material – particularly the files of the government departments – letters and all the local newspapers, which were perhaps the best source of finding out what was going on. They were just full of violence. It was quite clear from the material we uncovered that in the nineteenth century no one doubted that British colonisation was very violent, particularly in the second half of the century, when they were conquering northern Australia. People at the time talked openly about it. They said, *Well, we must. How else are we going to settle the country if we don't give these people a lesson they'll never forget?* It wasn't a debate about whether it happened, it was a debate about whether all that violence was necessary. It was about the morality of it, not the actuality. Eddie Mabo, Noel Loos and I also started recording oral histories. We'd go round and once Eddie had explained who we were, we were accepted.

Then I put it all together in *The Other Side of the Frontier* (1981). This was the book that established my reputation but also established a new sort of history. I offered it to Penguin Books in 1981 but they turned it down, saying there were 'too many books about Aborigines'. Quite astonishing! So we published it ourselves. Within no time we sold 5000 copies with no publicity, no marketing. Orders just came in. The History Department office became a book-selling place. Penguin then published a second edition.

The strong reaction against the book didn't come nearly as soon as I had expected and was undoubtedly related to the coming to power of John Howard in 1996. He very much took up the crusade against what Geoffrey Blainey had called the black armband view of Australian history. Howard believed this view of Australian history would make young people ashamed to be Australian, that history should give people pride in their country, that the history of Australia is all about resilient pioneers and settlers, and that black armband historians destroyed that story.

A few years ago, John Howard was making a documentary about Robert Menzies and the producer pointed out to him it was one-sided, given that he was just interviewing people who agreed with him. He suggested that Howard include a couple of people he didn't agree with. Howard chose Tom Keneally and me.

Howard interviewed me for several hours and I found him to be quite an engaging chap who, despite his hail-fellow-well-met bonhomie, had a hard, extremely calculating persona. He'd be looking at you and engaging pleasantly but you could see that he was really calculating. I found him fascinating.

To counteract the black armband view of history, Howard started an incredible crusade for commemorating war. He pointed to the great achievements of the Anzacs. As a result, a generation was brought up with the idea that war is our most defining experience, that Australia really began on the shores of Anzac Cove.

Noel Loos, Eddie Mabo and I often had lunch together at the university where Eddie was working as a groundsman. Eddie often spoke about his love for Mer (Murray), his island home. He had been expelled by the Queensland government as a teenager for mixing with troublemakers and communists and wasn't allowed to go back even for his father's funeral. I once said to him, 'Look, how do know that your land will still be there when you get back?' And he said, 'Everyone knows it's Mabo land.'

Noel and I discussed whether we should tell him, 'Look, mate, you don't own that land. It's all Crown land.' We decided we had to tell him, and he was aghast. The other thing I told him was that I thought he'd have a very good chance to win a court case, and this was partly because the Torres Strait land system was so different. Murray Island had only been claimed by Queensland in 1879 and was not part of the original British claim. I had a vague memory of famous cases in the American Supreme Court with the 'Indian' title cases of the 1820s and 1830s, so I said I reckon you'd probably win a court case, and if you do win, you'll become famous. Now, here was a comparatively unknown academic and a Torres Strait Island gardener talking over lunch. Who would have imagined!

Far less well known is the *Wik* case in 1996, which recognised that Aboriginal people in Australia had residual rights over land held under pastoral leases. The issue was no one knew the history. My research in British archives found evidence that the British Colonial Office in the 1840s created pastoral leases, which were in fact licences, that allowed for the mutual use of the same land. The British government was deeply concerned because it was obvious that Aboriginal peoples were being driven off their own country and that wasn't what they intended. So what they did was create a situation where all pastoralists had not a lease but a licence to pasture animals and keep people off land where there was actually cultivation. It meant that Aboriginal peoples had an absolute right to remain and live on their country and it was illegal to force them off their land.

When you looked at that, you realised that this was a profoundly different land tenure than people had thought. Out of the blue, the High Court made it clear that these pastoralists only had the right to run their animals and that the local Aboriginal peoples had parallel rights.

This was different to the principles set down in the *Mabo* case, whereby a lease extinguishes native title. Whether the situation would change after a lease expired is another argument, but the point was that these pastoral leases didn't give absolute rights to the pastoralists, which is amazing. And so many of the land-use agreements have been by people who would have difficulty proving native title or who just feel the process is so longwinded that it's much easier to come to a land-use agreement when you've got your rights under pastoral leases. So that, too, was extraordinary.

'I was blessed with a great deal from my background, but there was also a way of seeing, and a way of being, that I had to discover for myself.'

Anna Funder

Bearing witness to the past

I am inspired by a mixture of things, but if I look at the books I've written, I've been most fascinated by stories that haven't yet been told. In the case of my first book, *Stasiland* (2003), they were stories of ordinary people who resisted the German Democratic Republic (GDR) regime. Those stories weren't being told at the time, for interesting reasons. In the case of *All That I Am* (2011), it was the very earliest resistance to Hitler that hadn't been written about – and what happened to those brave people faced with British appeasement.

I don't think giving up my job as a lawyer was such a big turning point; I was always going to write. Probably for all creative people it's like that. It's part of your make-up and you must recognise it at some point and just do it. Other work I was doing felt false somehow – it felt like a deliberate avoidance of an engagement with the world, and with words, that was in my nature. Until I write something, I don't really understand it. I am skating on the surface of a reality which I need to pin down and represent before I can see what it really is.

I grew up in quite a high-powered family, a family interested in ideas and in social justice. We had an intense curiosity about the world, in its reality that could be proven scientifically, or sociologically, in demographic studies. Those kinds of truths were important. Other

TURNING POINTS

kinds, the sort that could perhaps be felt or intuited, which weren't evidence-based, were not so much currency in the family. For me, it was these other kinds of unseen truths that were fascinating. I was blessed with a great deal from my background, but there was also a way of seeing, and a way of being, that I had to discover for myself.

When I was a lawyer, I was interested in the way societies are set up constitutionally and politically to try to be fair, in an effort to curtail the human impulse to power that then tramples on other people. My background in human rights law and constitutional law became important in my writing in ways I couldn't have foreseen. In the GDR, the words 'human rights', 'democracy' and 'constitution' were bandied about – and there were even elections – but in fact that was all a sham. My training meant I could see this ersatz version of a constitutional democracy in its inner workings. *Stasiland* is personal – about me and the people in it. It's not a constitutional analysis! But I do think my legal background gave me courage when I was interviewing belligerent Stasi men who wanted to educate me about human rights and their 'humane' society behind the Berlin Wall. And when they pointed out flaws in democracies – so many poor people so vulnerable to rapacious capital, and so on – I could see that too.

The beginnings of *Stasiland* go right back to when I was a student at the Free University of Berlin in 1988, the year before the Wall fell. To experience living in a walled-in city deep inside the Eastern Bloc set me wondering about what was happening on the other side of that wall. I met people who had been expelled from East Germany, artists and writers mainly. I was forcibly struck by the questions: why did the German Democratic Republic want to get rid of its best and brightest? What sort of system has to get rid of dissent or the truth?

The GDR was a system that used fear to pressure people into betraying one another to the state so it could control them utterly. When I started interviewing people for *Stasiland*, it wasn't how dark their stories were that really struck me, it was admiration for how they survived as moral and psychological beings in an immoral world that tried to destroy them. I felt quite quickly, and I still feel now, that I was investigating extraordinary human conscience and courage: even in a closed universe like this, where the only way to survive is to betray those you love, a lot of people just will not do it, no matter the consequences for them. This is a fundamentally extraordinary thing about humans, and the resisters to the GDR regime allowed me to see it close up.

One of the questions underlying *Stasiland* was: if you remember something difficult, does it liberate you? In the case of psychological trauma, there are different theories. For example, to remember something of the pain of a memory, does that lessen the pain or does it reinforce that memory? I was of course implicated in this, as I was asking people to honour me with their stories. Was it cathartic for them? Was it a good thing to set down these truths for posterity, even when that might be damaging, now, to the people whose truths they were? That's a very open question and that's the question the book hinges on, because it is what it's doing.

But for a society, this issue becomes not one of personal psychology but of justice, and of the truth of history justice requires. The ex-Stasi and all the people aligned with them didn't want those stories to be told because they incriminated them. These were the voices of people they had formerly tried to silence. When I started my work, the prevailing view was 'Let's all put this behind us' and 'Let's all get over it and get along'. This was a move to silence the resisters and victims again, and to fabricate the innocence of the former ruling elite by trivialising its crimes. My answer was to tell the stories, enabling these people to be heard and, possibly, honoured.

At the launch of the book in Leipzig, a woman stood up and asked, 'Why does it take a foreigner to tell our stories?' Being foreign, especially Australian, was a privilege I hadn't fully understood when I was doing those interviews. The people I spoke to knew nothing about Australia. I could have been from Mars. Both the Stasi men and the resisters were very open with me. I could ask the most basic and apparently ignorant questions and they didn't roll their eyes and think what an idiot I was. That meant they would explain in great detail anything I asked about, from the Russian Revolution to the World War II, from the reconstruction of Germany to the foundation of the East German state. In doing this, their side of the story, whichever side it was, became really clear.

At that same book launch, there was a group of threatening-looking Stasi men sitting in the front two rows. After my reading they got up and walked out in a huff. At that moment another reason became clear to me why it took an outsider to tell these stories. The ex-Stasi are still around. They are in the supermarkets, the cafés, they are at the book launches. That makes it hard for former East Germans. You can't be certain that there won't be repercussions even now, if you speak out against this old cadre. That didn't apply to me. Mind you, some ex-Stasi sued me in Australia about something I'd said about their activities harassing former activists *after* the fall of the wall, so I knew I'd done something right.

When I started working on *Stasiland,* I wanted to write a novel based on Miriam's story, but it wasn't working. I looked at it and thought, *This material is too extraordinary to go in a novel.* If you're going to write a novel, you must create a believable world, and the world of East

Germany was simply not credible. Reality outstripped credibility, so the only way to do it was in nonfiction. Not only the world of the GDR and the perfidy of the Stasi but also the courage of people like Miriam was almost beyond belief. She had been imprisoned by the regime at the age of sixteen for distributing leaflets and was disowned by her family. Once I knew it was nonfiction, I had to work out how I was going to string it together, with all those separate stories. The world I was operating in to write the book was present-day Berlin, so I decided to use myself as a first-person narrator to depict the world I was writing in and the post-Stasi world of silence my interlocutors were living in.

There's something about telling the truth that is itself liberating. But the stories of the resisters were hard for them to tell, and hard to hear. They involved looking close-up at horror and the cruelty of human beings. In nonfiction there are no easy happy endings, but a book is a work of art and has to be beautiful. The task of *Stasiland* was to honour the stories faithfully and yet make a work as beautiful as it could be. When I say 'beautiful', I don't mean pretty or necessarily poetic, I mean an object with artistic value – which is to say one that can convey truths that are hard to look at if they're not in a satisfying form. The form elicits a kind of satisfaction a happy ending doesn't.

When I was at school, people here thought German was an odd and unfashionable language to learn and that Germany was a plodding place with bad food and terrible politics. But I loved living in Berlin in the 1980s and 1990s. I found it deeply fascinating, liberating, creative. The politics of West Germany was fair, and the people were making a serious attempt to look at their history in ways that we in Australia were not doing with our own history at that time. I found the Germans' relationship to culture and art and music and literature was central to their sense of being alive, and I felt the same.

TURNING POINTS

The first question I think about when I'm writing is: should it be fiction or nonfiction? I think not everybody asks themselves that question because most people set out, quite sensibly, to write one or the other. With *Stasiland*, I wanted to write a novel, but it just wasn't the right thing to do with that material at that time in history. It wasn't 'mine' to do what I wanted with. That material needed a work of witness. Once the decision was made, a whole lot of other aesthetic and ethical decisions flowed on from that about how to write something as powerful as possible involving real people.

With *All That I Am*, I was writing in the early twenty-first century about resistance to the Nazis in the 1930s. All the real people involved have died, and anybody who is going to be reading it thinks they already know a lot about that time and the politics and what happened. But the story takes place *before* the story that everyone thinks they know because it starts at the very beginning of the time when Hitler came to power. I'm writing of this group of privileged, cultured, often Jewish, but also not Jewish, people who saw better than anyone else what was coming. If I wrote that book today, post-Trump, it would be perhaps a different book again. Or possibly it's just that the way all dictators eliminate aspects of civil society and truth, and the people who represent them, is very similar. To read the novel is to see other things in it, things closer to us now. You might think you're writing history, but you're not really. Things in the mirror are closer than they appear.

So part of my writing process is asking: what do I *owe* the material and the people in it, and then, given the time and place of myself and my audience, how best should I acquit myself of that responsibility? These are questions based on a kind of guts and passion, love and admiration of the people I am writing about, as well as what I owe to readers whose time and empathetic attention I'm asking for. The advantage of basing a story on people who are no longer alive is that it's less intrusive to represent characters based on them and get inside their imagined psyches, a sort of bringing back to life that I wouldn't do to a living person. That meant that a novel was possible. The other reason was because it's not possible to absolutely know what went on in that room in the top-floor flat in Great Ormond Street, London, where the two young German women were found poisoned. Being able to imagine that based on real evidence is the work of *All That I Am*.

'I love to encounter an experiment that doesn't fit the way I think it should. It makes me think differently. That's where discovery comes from.'

Peter Doherty

Embracing the science of potential

Growing up in Queensland in the 1940s and 1950s, I was a totally naïve kid, a year younger at the local public school than most of my cohort, totally unsocialised. I grew up in a historic time in that my childhood was not that different from my parents'. That world has gone. I was seventeen before we got a television – a key factor.

Both my parents left school at fifteen. Mine was the first generation in our family to go to university. My mother, Linda Bayford, was a piano teacher who gave me an appreciation of and emotional need for classical music. My father, Eric Doherty, was a clever man frustrated by his lack of a formal education. He trained as a telephone mechanic and became an administrator involved in planning telephone services. He gave me a desire to learn and understand.

I had this non-conformist, socially aware Methodist upbringing, and my values are absolutely formed by that. There's nothing in that low church tradition about making money or being successful in that sense or exploiting other people. In fact, Methodists even believed insurance was gambling. It was a powerfully formative upbringing and the more I think about it, the more I think how much I'm a kind of slave to that. There's also a strong anti-authoritarian theme in my thinking. I can't stand authoritarians, dogmatic people and professional liars, which is why I find Trump so deeply loathsome.

Growing up without much money convinced me that I needed to get some sort of reasonable job. I thought about medicine, but the only doctors I knew were people who pretty much sat around in suburban offices listening to people whining. I didn't want to do that. As a gauche sixteen-year-old I had absolutely zero empathy.

I had a brilliant older cousin, Ralph Doherty, who was in the process of establishing himself as a leading viral epidemiologist and who went on to discover the Ross River virus. He did medicine and then trained in public health. I was influenced by him and thought research might be an interesting thing to do, especially research on diseases in domestic animals. There was a lot of furore at that time about feeding the world and I thought I would help feed the world.

What changed my life was going to an open day at the Queensland University Veterinary School, where I encountered biology for the first time. I had done physics and chemistry, though my natural inclinations were literature and history. I am passionate about history. One of the things that really disturbs me now is education. A lot of the rigour's gone out of it. Governments that are anti-history don't like the truth being exposed.

I was seventeen when I went to the open day. It was 1957. At the time the University of Queensland was one of only two places in Australia and New Zealand where veterinarians could train. As I wrote in my book *The Beginner's Guide to Winning the Nobel Prize* (2005), my interest was piqued by the demonstrations in embryology, anatomy and pathology, and by the rather scatty, sexy, chain-smoking young laboratory technician who looked after the displays. It was all so different from anything that I had ever encountered before. It looked real, interesting and doable. From that moment I was hooked on biology.

At the veterinary school of physical sciences, zoology, botany and biochemistry were taught by the science faculty and physiology by the medical school. Important influences on my thinking were the study of infectious diseases under John Francis and immunology under John Frederick Adrian Sprent and reading virologist Frank Macfarlane Burnett. I also discovered drinking beer and playing cards and graduated with a very undistinguished degree.

Because I was on a bonded scholarship, I had to go and work for the Queensland Department of Agriculture and Stock for a few years. As I expressed an interest in research, they sent me to the country to work as a rural veterinary officer. I covered long distances driving to post-mortems of cattle and pigs that had died of unknown causes and I diagnosed a disease called trichomoniasis, which they thought they had eliminated, so they were none too pleased.

The department had some research funds and brought me back to the state veterinary laboratory, the Animal Research Institute, in the Brisbane suburb of Yeerongpilly. This was when I started working seriously on infectious diseases. I became very interested in how infectious diseases work and discovered that I was good at what I was doing. That's pretty powerful. This was where I caught the bug. This was my turning point, my epiphany, what I gained from going down the path of veterinary science.

Being at Yeerongpilly was also a personal turning point, as I met microbiologist Penny Stephens there. We married in 1965. She has been enormously supportive and thinks a lot the way I do and keeps me in my place. She tells me off whenever I'm being really stupid, which is fairly frequently!

TURNING POINTS

In 1966, I gained my master's degree in veterinary science from the University of Queensland. I had been especially influenced by Macfarlane Burnett's work on immunology. Then a colleague told me about a visit he had paid to the Moredun Research Institute in Edinburgh, where they were doing major research on scrapie, a fatal degenerative disease affecting the nervous system in sheep and goats. The following week I saw a job in the Department of Experimental Pathology at the Moredun advertised in the back of the science journal *Nature*. They wanted an experienced veterinarian neuropathologist. I applied, telling them I didn't know anything much but was planning to do a PhD in pathology, and got a response saying 'come'. Apparently, they had no other applicants.

Penny and I sailed to Portsmouth, then went by train to Edinburgh via the *Flying Scotsman* in early 1967 and spent five happy years in Auld Reekie. It was a great experience even though we had very little money. From the start I did my own research. I enrolled as an external PhD student at the University of Edinburgh Medical School and was largely unsupervised. My subject was pathogenesis of louping-ill meningoencephalitis.

Before the birth of our two boys, James and Michael, Penny worked at the Institute of Animal Genetics. In the long vacation we would go camping around Europe and enjoyed the Edinburgh International Festival every summer. I've got very fair skin and living in Scotland was the first time I could spend all day outside and never get sunburnt. Scotland is sunnier now due to global warming. Edinburgh was wonderful but financially I couldn't see any way of getting ahead. We were always living in rented accommodation and I just didn't see how we could make a decent living there. But it was lovely, we loved Edinburgh.

A growing realisation that I had no real understanding of contemporary immunology led me to leave my research position in Edinburgh in December 1971 and take up a short-term fellowship in Canberra at the John Curtin School of Medical Research (JCSMR). It was during my time here that Rolf Zinkernagel and I made the discovery that would lead to us sharing the Nobel Prize more than twenty years later, in 1996.

Rolf was Swiss and had been working at the University of Lausanne on bacterial immunity. We first met in 1974 when he arrived at JCSMR to work with immunologists Bob Blanden and Gordon Ada. They were short of space so moved Rolf into the laboratory with me. All science now is very much a team effort, but it was just the two of us, a couple of young guys working together in a lab. It was quite an extraordinary set of circumstances that made me very independent professionally. Someone of that age (I was in my early thirties) coming into a research situation today would almost certainly end up in a research group and probably not get a lot of credit for their work, but we made the discovery about how the immune system recognises virus-infected cells by ourselves. It was a major turning point and paved the way for modern treatment strategies for cancer and vaccines.

We were very early in our careers. Although I'd been working in pathology and infectious diseases for some time, I had to learn basic immunology. Rolf had more formal training in that area but had little research experience. So we both came to immunology fresh, with no preconceptions. That sort of firing off one another was really important. It was as much a technical complementation as an intellectual one.

I had learned from reading Macfarlane Burnett to look at everything through the prism of teleological Darwinism, meaning if it doesn't fit natural selection, it's probably wrong. I love to encounter an experiment

TURNING POINTS

that doesn't fit the way I think it should. It makes me think differently. That's where discovery comes from. Nobel Prizes for science are awarded for discovery. It's only in science that you find out things that nobody has ever discovered before, and that's enormously satisfying.

In the field of biology, a lot of the Nobel Prizes are due to a chance discovery or looking into something and realising its potential. The Nobel Prize for Chemistry in 2020, for example, was awarded to two young women (they're in their fifties but that's young for me), Emmanuelle Charpentier and Jennifer Doudna. They were very good at their field, then investigated the science further, realised the potential and went for it, developing a method for genome editing. If I was to say anything to anyone about the secret of success, it would be don't dwell on it. Think about it for a bit, but do it now. Don't mess around. There are so many people I know who mess around forever and never get anything done.

Two short research reports Rolf and I published in 1974, together with a brief 1975 hypothesis article in *The Lancet*, were the basis of our being awarded the Nobel Prize. Publications in other leading journals, followed by speaking tours in Europe and the United States, meant that in the worlds of immunology and transplantation genetics, we went from total obscurity to fame – or, for some who could not grasp what we were saying, notoriety. With simple experiments that built on decades of work by others, in particular mouse transplantation geneticists, we'd discovered why humans have a transplantation system.

To be given the Nobel Prize a couple of decades after a discovery is not unusual. During that time, we won several major awards, but the Nobel is the pinnacle. One of the things that a lot of other prizes do is predict the Nobel, as it's the only one the media takes any real notice of. The Lasker Awards and the Canadian Gairdner Awards are the main predictors. The Lasker is the top American medical research prize, and when we were awarded that in 1995, we knew we were in the running for the Nobel.

Apart from the Lasker and the Nobel, the greatest scientific accolades were being elected to the Royal Society in 1987 then the US National Academy of Sciences (NAS) in 1997. Formed in 1660, the Royal Society is United Kingdom's academy of science and, indeed, is the oldest academy of science in the English-speaking world. New fellows sign a vellum (calf skin) book donated by King Charles II. The NAS was founded by Abe Lincoln during the American Civil War and is equally significant in the contemporary science scene.

The discovery we made in Canberra pushed me across into basic medical science and that meant that I didn't really fit the mould in Australia very well. If I'd been a medical graduate and I'd made that discovery I would have been welcomed with open arms, but there wasn't a great deal of interest here at the time, so I took a job in Philadelphia. We spent seven years there, during which time Penny developed a new career in drug information. In 1982, we returned to the JCSMR in Canberra. That didn't work out – you should never go back – and we ended up going to Memphis, Tennessee, in 1988, where I was offered the Chair of the Department of Immunology at St Jude Children's Research Hospital, a superb open research environment, extremely well funded.

My years at St Jude proved to be an extremely interesting time. It went from being an institution of 800 people to about 4000. It's connected to Hollywood and we got to know Robin Williams and other stars. The Research Hospital raises a billion dollars a year in public support.

I didn't want to retire in Memphis, so we decided to come back to Australia in 2002 – though I returned regularly to Memphis each year (until the outbreak of Covid-19) to collaborate on studies of immune T-cell effector function and memory. My main reason for returning was that I thought I could be helpful to Australian science. That proved to be completely wrong regarding climate change.

If you really want to make statements about Australia, you need to be like Germaine Greer. You go and live somewhere else, come back, deliver a blast and then get on a plane and go. You have to be outrageous. I'm not outrageous about medical science but I am outrageous about climate change. I am concerned that action will only be taken in catastrophic circumstances.

I have also been aware of the possibility of a pandemic for years. In 2011 I published *Pandemics: What Everyone Needs to Know*. It was part of a series commissioned by Oxford University Press. At first I thought the book should be written by a public health doctor or epidemiologist, and then I felt, well, if a lab scientist writes it, it will be a different book. It's fine, there's nothing wrong with it. It's held up pretty well, in fact, and it has recently been translated into two Chinese languages. I anticipated that a pandemic would cost trillions of dollars, which is true. What I didn't realise were the social consequences. I did warn the powers that be not to cut public health services and public health laboratories, which has happened all over the place. This was one of the reasons things went badly in Melbourne. There were lots of cuts to public health, but the lab was fine. In fact, the lab side in Victoria was terrific.

We need to learn every lesson we can from the Covid-19 pandemic. For instance, the mantra had always been because of the influenza outbreak that you can't stop these viruses by stopping the planes. But we know we contained the virus by stopping the planes, so one of the things we have to agree on globally is that as soon as something like this happens in a locality, the planes get shut down from that region. Another thing is that the Coalition for Epidemic Preparedness Innovations (CEPI), an international organisation started by Bill Gates, focused on developing vaccines in conjunction with the University of Queensland. We didn't actually need this because vaccines were coming to the fore from elsewhere. What we should have had is CEPI focusing on making anti-viral drugs. Anti-viral drugs work for influenza, anti-viral drugs work for HIV. We should have been making anti-viral drugs that would block all the coronaviruses, and others, against possible pandemic threats caused by the filoviruses and henipaviruses.

We've known for some time these viruses are out there, especially in bats. With only two 'common cold' coronaviruses circulating in humans prior to the year 2000, we've had five more jump across in the past two decades. Four of these are now in us with, in three instances, including SARS-CoV-2, global transmission across the planet. And there are many more potential threats in the massive bat wildlife reservoir. So we're going to get more pandemics, there's absolutely no doubt about it. We need to be prepared for that. Very likely they will be worse than this as far as diseases are concerned. If we have anti-viral drug cocktails to start with, we'd be in much better shape, as we know we can't get a vaccine out in less than a year.

Nonetheless, the world has come a long way. We didn't even isolate the first influenza virus from humans until 1933, fourteen years after the end of the 1918–19 influenza vaccine. And the first influenza vaccines weren't rolled out for populations at large until decades after World War II. Covid-19 is a disease we've never seen before; we've seen nothing like it. It's totally new. My interest has always been in how diseases work, so I'm fascinated by it. There's nothing that really mimics it in animals.

Before the pandemic I got into a mode where I was travelling far too much. I was exhausted all the time. It was becoming intolerable. I just stopped and thought, *As long as I don't catch the damn thing, it's probably saved my life.* Actually, it's caused me to do a lot of thinking. A large grant that I was involved with finished in December 2020, so I thought this was the time to retire. I do crude woodworking, which is a disease I caught from my father, I've been exercising a lot more, and Penny and I watch a lot of European murder mysteries. We watch people being murdered in all sorts of ways.

Winning the Nobel Prize put me on the public stage and changed my life. I'm in the unusual position of having two buildings (one in Edinburgh) named after me in my lifetime. One of the nice things about our Melbourne institute is that we're mixing medicos, diagnosticians and scientists working in infection, immunity, epidemiology and everything that characterises the study of, and the capacity to deal with, infectious disease. It's a great team of dedicated and highly professional people with an extraordinary and complementary mix of skills.

My non-conformist background has powerfully influenced my commitment to serving the community. I was brought up with the mantra: *Good, better, best. Never let it rest. 'Til your good is better and your better is best.* It can turn you into an obsessive neurotic. I'm not neurotic – just obsessive.

'It's now many years since I walked across the desert, but everything is, in a sense, crossing a desert.'

Robyn Davidson

Becoming the heroine of her own adventure

Walking from Alice Springs to the coast of Western Australia in 1977 changed my life. It was a turning point in that it took me from one track onto another – not just the trip itself but also because of what it generated.

I had no intention of writing about the trip. It was very personal, very private. I didn't think anyone would be interested and, in any case, it wasn't anyone else's business. I just wanted to be in the desert, and I knew I had to do something large enough to grow me up, to integrate myself as a person, because I was a pretty lost sort of kid. I did the journey with that in mind.

I began with zero skills, none whatsoever. Acquiring the camels, learning to train and look after them, took me two years. It was a very formative time and incredibly challenging. I had to be able to cope with things going wrong, fixing them, keeping on. There was a point before I left when I came close to abandoning the whole thing.

The camels took off one night. They just did a runner. Something spooked them; I had no idea what. I tracked them for a day and couldn't find them, couldn't find them, couldn't find them! A week passed. Some generous people in town with a light aircraft offered to take me up to see if we could spot them from the air. As we took off,

TURNING POINTS

I remember thinking, *My camels have gone, they'll be alright, I've done my duty towards them, now I can just go home. I don't have to do this thing. I'm free. I'm released.* And, of course, then we found them. That's when I realised that I was actually going to have to do it.

The journey itself was transformative in all sorts of ways, both predictable and unpredictable. I was able to shed stuff that wasn't important anymore or that was only important in a different context – a lot of psychological stuff, plus obsessions with time. There's a reason why we think of pilgrimages as meditative. Just walking on the earth, you go into a different mental state. You become aware of your surroundings in a quite different way and you become much more attuned to how things work and where you are in that pattern. It started to seem to me like I was just part of this web.

It took a long time to get to that kind of state or rhythm. I think if you're on your own walking and sleeping on the dirt like that every day, day after day, you're so attuned to the earth that you see things, you learn things, you notice relationships between things. But the mind is a dangerous thing. It can drive you bonkers or it can take you to better places.

It took me to a better place walking for a month with Mr Eddie, an Aboriginal Elder I met in the desert quite by chance. It was hugely important in a way I hadn't predicted. He couldn't speak English and I couldn't speak Pitjantjatjara. We laughed a lot. He taught me to let go of western preoccupations with time and structure. He was completely at home in his country, an existential at-homeness. After I left him and was on my own for a month, my brain wiring changed. I discovered the antithesis of loneliness.

I was utterly unprepared, however, for dealing with becoming a public person. The renown took me into worlds that otherwise I would not have been in. For example, after the trip was over, I think it was ten days later, I was in New York City.

When I had accepted the sponsorship deal with *National Geographic* to help me fund the trip, it felt like I'd sold my soul. It was an extraordinary time in Alice Springs politically and culturally, with the flow-on from those old 1960s politics. *National Geographic* was like the last word in conservative. I felt I was compromising myself on various levels. I hadn't wanted to get funding or anything like that. I wanted to do it on my own. For a while I worked in a pub at night trying to make enough to buy scraps to build saddles, but preparing for the trek took up all my time. At the end of that two years in Alice Springs, I'd trained myself, trained the camels, built a lot of the stuff I needed, but had no money. I needed $2000, which was a lot of money then. There was no other way I could get it. Through a friend I met a roving photojournalist, Rick Smolan, who turned up in Alice briefly and talked me into writing to *National Geographic* to ask for sponsorship. So I did, and they agreed. This meant I could buy the rest of the equipment I needed, but it also meant that a) I would have to have Rick taking photos at various points along the journey, which I hated the thought of; and b) I would eventually have to write something, which I had never intended to do.

So that's how I found myself when the trip was over, walking through the streets of New York, still seeing the world geologically and feeling I was in this landscape of strange canyon clusters and just thinking, *I'm the last sane person on earth. This is completely mad.* I'd never been outside Australia before. I had to write something for *National Geographic*, about 3000 words. They had thought they'd have to ghost it or get it out of me by talking, but I wrote it in a week, and they were gobsmacked. But I was shocked when they showed me how they'd edited it. They had me saying things like Eddie was the finest man, white or black, that I'd ever met, that sort of awful stuff. I crossed it out furiously, but they damped down what I'd written into a sort of geographic-ese, which was, of course, predictable.

I decided I couldn't let it stay at that, so I went home and wrote a much longer piece to claw back what I felt was the authenticity of what I had done instead of turning it into this shmucky dental-room magazine story. I wrote about 10,000 words, and I think it was Rick's agency, I can't remember, who sent it off to *The Sunday Times* in London and they printed it as a cover story. That story got syndicated to something like one hundred magazines around the world as a cover story, so suddenly, the persona of the Camel Lady was born.

It was disorientating for me, and my instinct was to withdraw. I didn't like being a public person. I hated the whole publicity aspect of it. I wouldn't have put it in these terms then, but I was very aware of how one's idea of oneself can be seduced and tainted by both praise and blame, so my instinct was to withdraw to protect what I felt was – I hate the word 'integrity' – but it was something like that. Something precious, something real to me that hadn't been distorted by other people's fantasies or versions or whatever.

Then I got a letter from Liz Calder, commissioning editor at Cape Publishers in London. She said, 'We've just read the piece you wrote in *The Sunday Times* – would you write a book for us?' And I thought that if I wrote a book, it would be like throwing a bone to the dogs. Instead of coming for me, they'd go for the book. So again, I was protecting myself. I felt that the world would have the book and people would leave me alone.

Meanwhile, I'd written to Doris Lessing as a fan and she, brilliant woman that she was, sort of smelt something in my letter. She wrote back and we started a correspondence. She suggested I go to London to write the book. So I went to London and ended up living in Doris Lessing's house. She was amazing and generous. I wrote the book (published as *Tracks* in 1980) and then, blow me down, it turned into a bestseller.

What I found interesting was that men liked it as much as women. Most of the reviews were written by men. They were fabulous, exciting and generous. Everybody who read the book seemed to get something from it that wasn't to do specifically with being female – it was more about the human spirit.

Women do, I think, find something about courage. Even though you're scared, even though you're inadequate, even though you're hopeless, even though you're whatever, if you just step forward into your life, wonderful things can happen. Of course, terrible things can happen too, but that's how it is. Things happen. And that idea still seems to resonate with people. Again, this theme was completely unconscious on my part in the sense that I just wrote what I wanted to write. I believe if you're true to yourself and just do what you do, with luck, that's what will resonate. People smell genuineness. In that sense, the trip utterly changed everything, but without my anticipating it.

One thing I hadn't expected was how strongly I felt about my camels. The relationship between humans and animals is, when you think about it, most mysterious. What is remarkable is that there can be cross-species communication, different bandwidths of consciousness whereby humans and animals can somehow make sense of each other and feel loyalty and affection towards each other. That's a very strange thing.

Each of the camels was very different in character and temperament. I'd trained the two males, Dookie and Bub, from when they were youngsters. I owe Kurt Posel, the owner of the first camel farm in

TURNING POINTS

Alice Springs, a lot because he just threw me into the work.[5] He was a very good teacher. He was also a nutbag! So, I knew my camels as characters, as entities. Dookie was a beast of genius. He had depth, was very knowing. Bubby was sort of silly. He was in love with Dookie, who was shy and adorable. Zeleika, the cow, had come in from the desert as an adult camel, so she was always much more wary, but very gentle. That was the gang. I could pick up their feet, crawl under their bellies, pull their tails, leap on them, hang off them, gallop them bareback. Amazing. The two boys were like pets; Zeleika was more mature and not so easily seduced. She was wiser than the other two put together in the ways of the wild. She was also pregnant, naughty little thing, and had a calf just before we set off. He was born a fighting handful and I called him Goliath. He was smart, cheeky, spoilt and demanding.

The journey brought that little group of animals much closer together. Who knows what goes on in a camel's mind when it's essentially relating to a primate as the leader of its group? It's very odd when you think about it, but we were very attuned to each other, all of us, including Diggity the dog, of course.

When the trip was over, I left the camels on a property in Western Australia. I spent hours saying goodbye. They lived there for five years. Then I brought them back to Alice Springs and let them loose in the bush – no ropes, no nose pegs, nothing. Just wild. Another five years later, I drove out to see them. I called them and their heads went up – they just couldn't believe it. It was amazing. I'd brought them watermelon and all their favourite things. I had a couple of hours canoodling with them and they remembered all the commands. I'd just whisper a command and they'd sit down or whatever. Then, when it was time to leave and I gave them a cuddle goodbye and headed off, they fell into line behind me. So, what's that? I think it's love.

It's now many years since I walked across the desert, but everything is, in a sense, crossing a desert. It's an ongoing process, it doesn't stop, ever, and it's not always onwards. You can go five steps forward and ten back, which I've done often in my life, believe me. But you can learn a lot from those ten steps back. You can learn a lot from failure and how to deal with failure. Probably you learn a lot more from failure than you do from success. I have one great quality and it has stood me in good stead – I am aware of the vast well of my own ignorance. So I'm always in a state of learning, always in a state of becoming, I guess, or of wanting to become.

'One of the things I really want to achieve in life
is to inspire other people with disabilities
to reach their goals.'

Anthony Bartl

Living without limits

The toughest turning point in my life happened when I was six years old. I was coming home from school one day and heading for a friend's house when I was struck by a speeding car. I was running a little late and didn't check for cars when crossing the road. I was knocked unconscious and flung in the air. My spine broke at the highest level. When you break your spine at that level, known as Cervical 1 or C1, you stop breathing. When that happens, you're not going to survive for long without oxygen to the brain. I had three minutes to live.

We lived close to a health centre and it so happened that one of the doctors there was walking past at the exact moment the accident happened. He rushed over and gave me mouth-to-mouth resuscitation till the ambulance came. If it wasn't for him, I wouldn't be here, or I'd be seriously brain-damaged, without the quality of life that I have now.

While the paramedics were frantically working on me, I had a near-death experience. I rose out of my broken body and kept rising higher and higher. Looking down, I could see all the commotion going on below but felt a real sense of peace and stillness. I found myself in a dazzling white hallway. I looked around in awe and started walking down a corridor between two lines of people forming a guard of honour on either side of me. I thought at first they were police then realised

TURNING POINTS

maybe they were my ancestors. They exuded love and I sensed they were protecting me. I kept walking until I came to a small doorway, hesitated, and was racked with indecision. I thought that if I went through that doorway, there might not be any coming back, that I would really be dead.

Curiosity triumphed. I opened the door and found myself in a dark room. It seemed to be empty, with streaks of light trying to break through in the corners. I felt that beyond that room was heaven itself. Then on the far side of the room I saw a man lying on a stretcher. His eyes were shut and I thought he was dead. As I went over to him, his eyes flicked open and he said, 'My name is Jesus. You are going to live beyond this traumatic time and have a long and prosperous life.' He had a reassuring, calm presence. We were a church-going family, so I knew who Jesus was. He was sending me back. I was filled with gladness and awe. I woke to find myself lying on my side in the intensive-care unit at the Royal Children's Hospital in Melbourne. Out of the window I could see several hot-air balloons floating past in the distance.

Before my accident I used to get as much out of life as I could. I'm a positive person: I was born that way. I always ran everywhere and at weekends used to go on walks on my own. I wasn't a homebody – I used to have all these adventures. I just loved using my body to its full potential. I remember that when I went to kindergarten, the thought often used to go through my head that I shouldn't be there because I felt so much older than the other kids. I felt I didn't belong there. I was in a hurry to grow up.

I learned later that my parents were put under a lot of pressure in the hospital to turn the ventilator off. They explained to me what had happened to my body, that I couldn't breathe for more than a few seconds on my own, that I would have no quality of life. Because of my injuries I couldn't talk, so they said that if I wanted to go to heaven, to blink once; if I wanted to stay, to blink twice. Apparently, I blinked and blinked and blinked. After my near-death experience, there was no way I wanted to die. I believed I could live a good life, that the world's an amazing place, although to change from being an active child with a real zest for life to being completely incapacitated was hard.

I was in the Royal Children's Hospital for two years, partly to get used to my injuries, to have rehabilitation and physio, and partly because my parents were fighting tooth and nail with the Transport Accident Commission to secure the support I needed to cope with my disability at home. They were pioneers in this at a time when the needs of people with disabilities were rarely considered. One of the things they did was to find a more suitable house, with wide corridors for wheelchair access and extra rooms to give me the space I needed, like a room for my carer, a bedroom and study for me, and a room for all my equipment.

I gradually regained the capacity to speak and adjusted to life. I was in bed for the first year in the Children's Hospital but the second year I had a wheelchair and started going to the hospital school, which was fantastic. I also started coming home every night for dinner and then every second weekend. I was anxious about living back home again without the comforts of hospital, where all the supports were. I couldn't breathe without the ventilator; I couldn't feel or move anything below my neck. That's the nature of C1 quadriplegia.

The most significant turning point for me after the accident was learning to accept my disability. It was a slow process. Until I was eight I was pushed in a manual wheelchair, which I found debilitating. A key change was when I got an electric chair and so was able to manoeuvre the wheelchair. It took me three months to learn how to use it. I could drive it with my chin, using a joystick attached to a frame in front of my chest. My ventilator was kept in a cage at the back of the wheelchair. It was a large unit – about thirty by forty centimetres – and very noisy.

After I returned home, I tried to go back to my old school, Holy Rosary Primary, but they wouldn't take me. It was a horrible shock – total discrimination and my first taste of life not being so easy with a disability. My parents approached the local state primary school in Kensington, and it was really accepting. I thrived there. I had an attendant carer and they built ramps for me to get to the classrooms.

When I finished primary school, I went to Marcellin College in Bulleen, which was also very accepting of my disability. On leaving school, I did a writing course at Victoria University, then did another writing course at RMIT and then studied for a Bachelor of Media Studies. I also did a teaching degree.

When I was eighteen, I got a phrenic nerve pacer instead of the ventilator, which I only use at night now. The phrenic nerve pacer sends electric impulses to the diaphragm through surgically implanted electrodes. It changed my life, giving me increased mobility. It also meant I didn't look so disabled, with tubes hanging off me, and didn't sound so much like Darth Vader, exhaling and inhaling blows of air noisily. The wheelchair I have now I got a year ago. It is the most sophisticated and flexible one yet. Its features include being able to lower it so I can put my knees under the table and be part of a group in a way I couldn't before. I can also raise it up and look people in the eye. I operate this via buttons in my headrest. One of the challenges for people in wheelchairs is not being able to climb stairs, though there are some wheelchairs that can now do this, which allows for more independence.

I am incredibly lucky to have strong family support around me and, thanks to the Transport Accident Commission, my twenty-four-hour care, my pharmaceuticals, my wheelchair and my computer are paid for. I also have a van adapted for my use that my carers drive. It means I am pretty independent. In fact, I love pushing my body to its limits and try to do as many things as possible. I've been snorkelling on the Great Barrier Reef, skiing at Falls Creek, hang-gliding and even horseriding. I've also driven a boat with my chin down at Docklands.

I love being around people – I love challenging my disability. When I go to hear music in pubs with my friends, I like to join the dancers on the dance floor. I especially love singing karaoke. My favourites are 'Never Tear Us Apart' by INXS and 'Suspicious Minds' by Elvis.

The most challenging thing I have done so far is go on a trip to South Africa in 2013. It was the realisation of a dream. I'm a big nature lover and always wanted to go on safari. It took me ten years to organise – to overcome all the hurdles, such as finding the right carers, finding a company that would agree to insure me, covering the cost. I had to have five carers with me and my usual insurance company refused to pay for this. That was my biggest barrier.

In 2010 I won $50,000 on Eddie McGuire's game show *Millionaire Hot Seat* and that money paid for my carers. The footage is on YouTube.[6] It was pretty daunting: bright lights shining in my face and Eddie right there in front of me. I was the first person with quadriplegia to appear on his show. My question was, 'What was the name of the rock band fronted by Jack Black?' I'm a big music fan and couldn't believe my luck. There were thousands of questions that could have come up that I couldn't have answered but I knew the answer to this one was Tenacious D. The audience stood up at the end and gave me a standing ovation. Eddie said it was one of the best shows he's hosted. I later lobbied Eddie for an extra $50,000 so that I could take a filmmaker with me and make a documentary. Contributions also came from the Pratt Family, the Collingwood Football Club Foundation, Triple M's 'Hot Breakfast' and the Robert Rose Foundation.

It was a great, great trip. We were away for two weeks, breaking the journey to Durban with stopovers in Sydney and Johannesburg. Apart from problems with the wheelchair owing to wear and tear, it was marvellous. It was the experience of a lifetime. As well as seeing fantastic wildlife, I spoke to the disabled kids at Khulani Special School and told them my story. I wrote the film and directed it. It's called *Unwheel Adventures* (2021) and premiered at Crown Casino.[7]

One of the things I really want to achieve in life is to inspire other people with disabilities to reach their goals. There's a lot of stigma out there if you're in a wheelchair. I see it when I do something as basic as going to a shop and the person behind the counter doesn't look at me – they look at the person with me, the carer, and say, 'What does he want?' I've given many disability awareness talks to educate people. I initiated a program with the Moonee Valley City Council, I wrote letters to schools to alert them to the fact I give these talks and followed up with a phone call. It's really rewarding as the perceptions able-bodied kids have of kids with a disability isn't generally very positive. This is on top of kids with disability themselves not having great self-esteem about their state.

People with a disability often get depressed and think nothing will change, but it's important to have an open mind about what's possible in the future and think ahead, think of the long term rather than the here and now. It's important not to let your attitude be a barrier. What I say to people struggling with their disability is to focus on the movement they've still got, to think of the good things and what might be available in the world to help them achieve. The hardest part is starting to think that way. You must keep pushing yourself.

I've been in the media on numerous occasions, especially on radio. I've made videos you can see on YouTube. My aim is that through all the things I've done, other people with disabilities will see that life goes on and you can still do a lot. I think I can offer hope, that I can show them that I've done all these things and that with a positive, can-do attitude, you can achieve a lot more. Even with a severe disability, a rich life is still possible.

'I suspect what people saw in me was a person who championed issues that others didn't.'

Fiona Patten

Learning about sex, drugs and the electoral roll

I never thought that I would be a politician, never in my wildest dreams. Yet the big turning point in my life was the first time I ran for parliament in the Australian Capital Territory elections in 1992. I didn't do it to be elected, I did it to give a platform to a whole range of ideas.

I was cajoled into running by my future partner, Robbie Swan, then a lobbyist for the Adult Video Industry of Australia. The industry wanted a woman to stand on a civil liberties ticket that would focus on porn and prostitution. It was also about freedom of trade and freedom of expression. I came to their notice because I was manager of the sex worker outreach group Workers in Sex Employment (WISE), and a member of the Australian Federation of AIDS Organisations. Both positions involved looking out for the welfare of sex workers and promoting sex education to the broader community.

At the time Robbie approached me I was twenty-seven, living in a share house in Canberra, seeing a really nice guy and planning to go to Queensland to set up a fashion business with my best friend, who was getting married. Over a period of seven to ten days we got evicted from the house because the friend I was sharing with hadn't been paying the rent, I broke up with my boyfriend and I agreed to run for parliament. I was also making my best friend's bridesmaid dresses and wedding dress. I ended up moving my sewing machine into my office, sleeping on the floor of one of the other bridesmaids' houses, and trying to work out what to do running for election for the first time.

Before then, if someone had asked me about going into politics, and lots of people did, I would say, never – never would I go into politics. I suspect what people saw in me was a person who championed issues that others didn't. They saw me as brave, talking about topics nobody else would. But I didn't see myself that way, although I have always been interested in other people and have enjoyed getting out there among lots of people.

That first election, I ran with the Hare-Clark Independence Party. There were three of us: Craig Duby (Minister for Finance and Urban Services), a Thai Buddhist monk and me. We became known as the drunk, the monk and the spunk.[8] Robbie's place became my team's centre of operations during the three months we had for campaigning.

Election day was 15 February 1992. It was one of those moments when you fall into something and it becomes a passion. We knew by 10.00 pm that we weren't going to win but I learnt later I had got the fourth-highest vote. Even though we didn't win a seat, we achieved what we had set out to do – got some great coverage during the campaign and moved some government policies in the ACT forward.

Running for parliament and meeting Robbie at that time and falling in love with him really did change things. Robbie and I started talking about what we could do together and that's when we established the Eros Association, an incorporated, not-for-profit organisation serving people working in the adult industry. They were denied access to a union so Eros combined representation, education and service provision, as well as advocacy and lobbying. It was the only incorporated adult industry association in the world, and I was elected the first president. It was a great training ground for politics.

I think my upbringing made me open to saying yes to opportunities. My father was an officer in the navy and for the first ten years of my life he was mostly away at sea. He really wasn't there. There's a family story about us meeting him coming off his ship when I was two or three. I was so excited he was coming home and ran down to this crowd of sailors. Apparently, I seemed to know exactly who my father was and grabbed this man round the knees. Of course, I grabbed the wrong man but fortunately my father wasn't far behind.

We were probably very fortunate that my mother had travelled a lot with her parents and changed schools often until she was sent to a French convent boarding school at the age of eight. We moved a lot because of my father's work, and it helped that my mother was used to moving around. She'd make any house we moved into a home: making the curtains wherever we went, doing those sorts of things. She encouraged me and my sister to be open to making new friends; she taught us that sitting waiting for someone to like you wasn't going to work.

Mum was a very strong person, very emotional. She carried the family. She wouldn't take any rubbish from us. She had a stiff-upper-lip, just-get-on-with-it approach to everything. She was the tour director, encouraging us to do lots of activities, to get involved in everything. Every weekend straight after swimming competitions we'd be in the campervan going somewhere for the weekend. She had great joie de vivre.

TURNING POINTS

Dad was also a big influence. He was gregarious, he loved to party. I've been reading some of the letters he wrote his parents; there's an extraordinary honesty in them, and humour. It's unexpected to hear him speak so frankly. I assumed they had a much more formal relationship. I see a lot of myself in him.

It's a sadness for me that Mum and Dad didn't get to experience my political success. Mum especially would have loved it. She would have come into my office and helped organise things. Because of her I never felt that I wouldn't fit in to a new environment or work situation. Her strategies from my childhood were particularly useful in my first few months when I was finally elected to parliament.

A big step on the way was starting the Australian Sex Party in 2009. It was in response to a proposal by Senator Conroy, Labor's Minister for Communications, to take censorship of the internet to a new level by introducing forced filtering of internet service providers. I contested the seat of Higgins in Victoria and won more than 3 per cent of the vote. Even then I didn't expect to get elected. It was again to give a platform to the issues, to show that some of them mattered to people – whether it was marriage equality or assisted dying or internet censorship. We would take the issue to the ballot box and people could vote. It would be a protest vote but would show that people cared about these issues. We got such great coverage in 1992 we thought we could do that again. And we did.

In 2010, I stood for the Senate in the federal election. It was the first Australia-wide campaign for the Sex Party, and we won more than 2 per cent of the national Senate vote. We came within 10,000 votes of the Family First Party for the Senate in Victoria.

Although I claimed then that we were the major minor party in Australian politics, it wasn't till the 2013 federal election campaign,

60

when I was the Sex Party candidate for a Senate seat in Victoria, that I saw myself as a politician. By then I really wanted to get elected, and in 2014 I contested the Northern Metropolitan Region in the Victorian Legislative Council and won.

I was surprised how easily I found my way around the job, though I shouldn't have been because I had spent all that time at the Eros Association as a lobbyist and poring over bills and legislation. I understood the process and I think I probably understood the notion of never letting the perfect get in the way of the good, that this was always the art of compromise. I think I was surprised that I felt like a natural. And well before the Eros days it was as though I was in training for politics. Around 1990, when I started working for WISE, we were brave, working on HIV and achieving remarkable things. The ACT government was really open to new ideas and all of a sudden I had an opportunity to influence legislation. I was talking to members of parliament about what sort of law reform there should be. All these politicians were new – they had only been in the job a matter of months – so we were all learning together about what consultation looked like, how to lobby, how to change the law, how to negotiate, how to communicate. It was an extraordinary incubator for us all.

That first year in the Victorian Legislative Council in 2014, I was nervous every time I stood up in the chamber to speak, but the biggest challenge was getting my head around so many issues. I had honed my skills on certain subjects and was great on sex work and censorship but now I was being asked to consider legislation on issues such as the sale of the Port of Melbourne. I had to find ways to train myself to understand these issues, to ask the right questions and understand the detail of the bills we were being required to pass.

I take my role very seriously. I don't really overlook any legislation. I do the background reading, I ensure that I understand it, that I know what I'm voting on. That adds to the workload enormously. I can go into the chamber and sit next to one of my parliamentary colleagues and they won't have a clue what bill's on or what they're voting for because they don't have to. They vote the way they're told, whereas for an independent like me, our votes can be deciding votes. I am currently one of five crossbenchers and we hold the balance of power.[9]

While the workload is much larger for an independent MP, the reward is greater, I think. I'm never going to be a premier, I'm never going to be a minister because I'm not part of a major party, but I'm always going to be able to vote with my conscience.

I am proud of the impact I have had politically. For instance, I was the first leader of a political party to call for a royal commission into child sex abuse in religious institutions. I instigated Australia's largest public inquiry into drug law reform, safe access zones for abortion clinics and introduced the bill which eventually led to the establishment of a medically supervised safe injecting room in North Richmond.

I am particularly proud of the work I did on the assisted dying laws. I still get emotional when I think about those laws and the process we went through to achieve them. I don't think anyone thought it was possible. I don't think anyone believed that when we put up the motion in 2015, we would be voting on it two years later.

In August 2017, reflecting our expanding horizons, we formally changed the name of the Sex Party to the Reason Party. We chose 'reason' because it is the single most important human faculty that is lacking in our parliament right now. I know that, as a small party, the time is coming when I need to step aside to let another person take the reins.

I sometimes wonder what if, in 1992, I had moved to Cairns and set up a fashion business with my best friend. I probably would have met a boy up there, probably would have married and led an incredibly different life. Instead, I am one of the first women in Australia to have started her own political party and then been elected. It feels good.

'My approach to life is to live simply
so that others may simply live.'

Gabrielle 'Didi' Dowling

Caring for the children

I was thirty-three when I was sent to Mongolia. It was 1993 and for some years I had been a nun with Ānanda Mārga, a spiritual organisation and philosophy founded in India in 1955 by philosopher and linguist Prabhat Ranjan Sarkar. My commitment meant being of service to people in different countries round the world, including Taiwan and India.

I had been living in Japan, teaching English in a small school. An Ānanda Mārga nun had set up this school and I had taken it over. It was a place for children who didn't fit in with normal schools there, which were very strict. Nuns and monks within Ānanda Mārga don't get paid, so to make some money I taught English after hours, as well as giving yoga and vegetarian cooking classes at weekends and running a collective meditation group. There were a couple of Ānanda Mārga monks living in Ulaanbaatar, the capital of Mongolia. They had been there since 1990 and had asked for a nun to come and work with them and teach yoga and meditation. My visa in Japan was running out, so I was chosen to go.

I knew nothing about Mongolia other than it was a very poor country emerging from almost seventy years as a Soviet state with close links to Russia. I was told I had to be self-sufficient – to find money to get myself there and support myself once I arrived. With Ānanda Mārga you could be sent somewhere that had an established structure in place or somewhere you had to work things out for yourself.

It was some months before I was able to go to Mongolia as there were complicated visa issues and I had to raise some money. I went to Taiwan, where Ānanda Mārga had a strong following. I used to go out with some Taiwanese members, and we'd chant in the street and collect donations in a can.

I arrived at Ulaanbaatar in winter and was totally unprepared for the cold. The temperature could drop to minus forty degrees. The monks had arranged for me to live in a local kindergarten that had some spare rooms. It was a large building that smelled of meat. I had been a vegetarian since I was fourteen and found the smell overwhelming. Everything smelled of boiled meat – even the money. I paid my rent by teaching English classes. English had become the country's second official language instead of Russian with the end of communism, so there was a demand for it.

Under communism, the government guaranteed the essentials of life and provided many different services for free. With the withdrawal of Russian involvement and trade in the late 1980s, Mongolia's economy collapsed. Under communism, people had not been allowed to own their own businesses or mine Mongolia's rich resources, such as copper and uranium. These were exploited by Russia. It was a time of great change, of great need. A lot of institutions, such as hospitals, closed. As much of the food came from Russia, there were large food shortages and extreme poverty.

Until then, kindergartens in Ulaanbaatar were basically free childcare centres catering for poor families, with many of the children living there during the week. If you were a single mother or very poor, you could bring your child in on Monday morning and pick him or her up late on Friday. It was a system that worked well if you had no transport and found it hard to get to the kindergarten each day in time to pick up your child. With the fall of communism, the government couldn't support these kindergartens anymore and suddenly families had to pay, which most couldn't, so enrolments dropped dramatically.

I wasn't involved with the running of the kindergarten where I lived but I used my space in the building to give meditation and yoga classes. People also came for blessings and to ask advice. I guess I tried to help in any way I could. I worked independently of the monks.

There was a playground next to the kindergarten where teenagers used to gather during the day. I often went and sat with them, and as I got to know them, they would ask me for water. My clients interpreted for me as I didn't speak Mongolian. I also gave them food and provided pencils and paper for drawing. I assumed they went home at night, so imagine my shock when I discovered that they were in fact sleeping curled up under bushes in the playground. They weren't welcome at home and they were expected to fend for themselves. Apparently, many of their parents spent most of their time at meeting places in the city where people would get together and drink vodka. There was a lot of domestic violence and alcoholism.

Life for girls in Ulaanbaatar, I learned, was much harder than for boys. Boys would steal and it was fun unless they were caught and sent to jail. It was obvious what was happening to the girls. They would invariably end up in sex work. There was a vulnerability about them because of their lack of education. It seemed their mothers told them nothing about the facts of life. I remember talking to one fourteen-year-old about being careful not to get pregnant. She told me she couldn't have a baby because babies are big and she was small. 'A baby

TURNING POINTS

couldn't fit in me,' she said. She went on to say she had about thirteen boyfriends who all loved her. She talked in a very innocent way about her lifestyle. It was so sad.

If it was too cold to sleep in the playground, the kids told me, they would go underground. Apparently many, many people slept there. There are three huge coal-fired power stations in Ulaanbaatar, which cause heavy pollution, covering buildings with grey dust. They pump hot water underground via large, insulated pipes all around the city, servicing apartments and other buildings. It's a huge network. People would make their way down to the pipes by pulling up culverts in the street and crawling into the tunnels. As well as the insulated hot water pipes, there were pipes carrying sewerage, which made it extremely unhygienic. I could see that the kids had a lot of infections as well as scabies and lice. I had some homeopathic medicines with me, which helped me heal their infections. Getting rid of the lice and scabies was a challenge, but we did it.

Sometimes street kids got work in the markets carrying things, but mainly they had to beg and steal and prostitute themselves to survive. When they started to visit me, my yoga students protested that they were dirty, smelly and bad, that I shouldn't be around them, but I felt I had to do more for the kids than just give them food and clothes and fix their infections. They needed safety and hope; they needed to be off the streets and safe. I discovered there was a government orphanage that accommodated abandoned kids, but it was limited to orphans: kids who went there for help had to produce their parents' death certificates to prove their orphan status.

I started visiting the parents of street kids where I could and telling them that they needed to look after their kids, that the way their children were living was dangerous. I always had at least a couple of my Mongolian students with me to interpret. They came to really care for the street kids.

Mostly it was hopeless. Almost invariably the family structure had broken down. The reasons varied and included poverty, alcohol addiction, homelessness, separations and simply a lack of love. The parents couldn't take the children back even if the kids wanted to return, which often wasn't the case. A few did go back to their families, but not a lot. It was clear the families had been affected by poverty and alcohol. Five of the girls ended up living with me, sleeping on mats on the floor.

My path to become a nun was circuitous. I grew up in Mulwala, in New South Wales, in a large Catholic family. I am dyslexic and found schoolwork difficult. I was slow at reading and writing and always failed exams. I was one of those kids who would write poems about my feelings and spend a lot of time daydreaming. I didn't really like the church and was looking for something different. The Young Christian Students Association appealed to me, and when I was thirteen or fourteen I ran a small youth group, which I loved, especially the summer camps.

I stayed at school till Year 11 even though I wanted to leave. I didn't want to spend my life living in the country, which would inevitably mean marrying one of the local boys – so I left home on my eighteenth birthday. For years I lived in share houses, did different jobs, travelled. I worked with young people at the YWCA in Melbourne, with people with disabilities at Willsmere Hospital.[10] I was deeply concerned about the care of the environment and hitched to Queensland to take part in a walk from the Queensland border to Sydney to protest sand mining.

TURNING POINTS

When I discovered I was pregnant, I left Australia and went fruit picking in New Zealand. My daughter, Sarah, was born there. It was an open adoption, so I met her adoptive parents. Giving Sarah up was very hard, and I took my time before going through with it. A few years later, I went to visit her with my parents. They fell in love with her and in fact she developed a good connection with them and with my family, which continues.

I first encountered Ānanda Mārga when I was twenty-one. At a Down to Earth festival in country Victoria, I met an Ānanda Mārga nun who told me that the Ānanda Mārga philosophy was self-realisation and service to humanity. They ran free schools and kindergartens, taught yoga and meditation and ran disaster relief programs. All this appealed to me, as my approach to life is to live simply so that others may simply live. I also liked the fact they were vegetarians. I offered to help them at a small school they had in Melbourne, where most of the kids came from the housing commission flats. I've always loved working with kids and remember thinking that this was more constructive than protesting.

I decided to study the Ānanda Mārga philosophy and spent some time at an isolated place owned by Ānanda Mārga near Gympie, in Queensland. I went with a friend and we both felt the amazing vibration of that land. It was like stepping through clouds. There was a small creek and a patch of rainforest and a pool big enough to swim in. The accommodation was a small tin shed, very basic. When my friend left, I was there on my own. It was the first time I lived by myself, and I loved it. I studied yoga philosophy and meditation and baked bread on the wood stove.

At first, I had no intention of becoming a nun, but something about this place made me change my mind. So I trained in Sweden and India.

Training lasted two years and followed a strict schedule of meditation, philosophy and yoga classes, beginning at 4.30 in the morning. There were about twenty-five of us and, when we were ready, we were given postings in different parts of the world. We were also given a new name. Mine was Didi Ananda Kalika. 'Kalika' means the beauty within. 'Didi' – which everyone in Mongolia calls me – means 'sister'.

After a while, the people running the Mongolian kindergarten asked me to leave as too many street kids were coming to see me and they didn't like it. I rented a place in an apartment block nearby, but the neighbours complained that I brought these 'rotten' kids round and gave the place a bad reputation. They hated it.

I decided I had to buy somewhere where I could offer these lost teenagers food and refuge. On the outskirts of Ulaanbaatar there were cheap places known as ger villages. *Ger* is the Mongolian name for yurts.[11] The streets were littered with rough stones and broken glass, electricity was often cut off, there was no plumbing and only drop toilets. I asked my yoga students to look for a house for me in that area while I went back to Taiwan to raise the money. While I was there, one of the local papers published an article about what I was trying to do for the street kids, which attracted some generous donations. My students found a family house in Yaarmag, a ger village about ten kilometres outside Ulaanbaatar. The house had one outside drop toilet and no running water, but I was able to buy it. Most Mongolian houses then had no bathroom or running water.

It was 1995, my second year in Mongolia, and here in this house I founded the Lotus Children's Centre. I started with these five girls and a little boy of two and a half who had been left behind when the government orphanage closed. He had been terribly neglected, was in bad health and disabled. I took him in before we moved and looked after him. We didn't have much furniture in the house, but then we didn't have the space. We all slept on mats on the floor. The lack of running water made it extremely hard to keep everyone clean.

Within weeks more children came, mostly younger. Some simply knocked on my door, while babies were left on my doorstep. The police brought me a girl of about one and a half who had been abandoned and very neglected. Then they came back with her baby sister and asked me to take her too. I realised I had seen their mother begging in the market and went and found her, but she refused to take either of the children.

I ended up with lots of babies of all ages, as well as older children and teenagers. Some of my yoga and meditation students, mostly in their late teens, moved in with me and helped with the babies. Part of meditation practice is serving others, which they took seriously. They had to change their opinions a lot.

One premature baby we looked after had a hole in the heart and died. Infant mortality was high in the area. In the winter pneumonia was common, but in the summer the problem was diarrhoea, caused by the drop toilets and lack of hygiene. Another source of sickness was the nearby coal-fired power station and its shocking pollution. We were also extremely overcrowded, and the place wasn't hygienic enough. Washing with no running water was a bit wild. I worried about how to improve our living conditions.

Many of the children I was caring for had rickets so were delayed in their walking. Others were suffering from a variety of illnesses, including syphilis, meningitis and malnourishment. I tried to enrol the older children at the local state school, but the teachers wouldn't take them. They thought they would be trouble. One child was accepted at a local school for disadvantaged children. I did my best to teach the other children myself.

About a year after setting up the Lotus Centre I met Jenni Storey, an Australian journalist who was working as a volunteer on a local English paper in Ulaanbaatar. She told me that Ric Smith, Australian ambassador to China and Mongolia, was giving a cocktail party in a few days at a city hotel for the handful of Australians living in Ulaanbaatar and suggested I should go.

To get there I had to take the bus. It was winter and freezing cold, so I was wearing my thickest, warmest outdoor clothes. It was hot in the hotel, but I couldn't take my warm things off as I wasn't wearing anything presentable underneath.

At the reception, an Australian man asked me what I was doing in Ulaanbaatar and I told him about the Lotus Centre. I didn't realise he was the ambassador. He asked if he could come and see for himself, which he did a few days later. He was really moved by what he saw and heard and asked me what I needed. I said I needed a bigger, better house, I needed running water and I needed heating. He arranged with AusAID (the Australian Agency for International Development) to give me $50,000. It was a lot of money and enabled me to build a larger house, drill for water and put in toilets. It transformed the children's health. Our new place was formally opened by Ambassador Ric Smith in November 1999.

As more and more babies were brought to the Lotus Centre and older kids in trouble of one sort or another found us, it was miraculous how volunteers came to help me care for these children. They invariably became very attached to the kids. One volunteer who made a great impact was a Scottish woman, Ishbel Ford, who had come to work in a kindergarten in Ulaanbaatar via the British charity Voluntary Service

TURNING POINTS

Overseas. She didn't like the place she'd been sent to and heard about the Lotus Centre. She asked me if she could work with me. I was in the process of setting up a kindergarten and she took this on and trained teachers to run it. She was brilliant and stayed with us for six years. She also helped with the education of the teenage girls, most of whom had never been to school. Laurie Beck, an Australian nurse, worked as a volunteer for two years and was also invaluable. Another extraordinary volunteer was Arjuna Erdenbaatar, a young male student who was crucial in helping me set up the Lotus Centre – the paperwork was extremely complicated. Tragically, he drowned some years later.

After we had been in Yaarmag for sixteen years, I decided we had to move. By then we had more than one hundred kids at the Lotus Centre; it was too crowded. We bought ten acres in a nicer and much cleaner area on the other side of town. Here we have been able to build better accommodation and sports and outdoor play facilities. We have also built two greenhouses, which not only provide us with vegetables but offer training opportunities for our older kids. Our children are getting a better education: some have gained scholarships to local private schools, some go to the local primary school, some are at a special-needs school, some are going to a Chinese-speaking school and others to a German-speaking school.

Mongolia has lovely summers that last about three months. The days are long and not too hot. The children always have three months' holiday, so we began an annual tradition of camping by a river about seventy kilometres from Ulaanbaatar. We hired some trucks, pulled our gers onto the back and took off. We stayed a couple of months and had a wonderful time. One of our many activities for the children was running 'virtual' workshops with volunteers from all over the world, in addition to our regular workshops in English language, dance, drama, cooking and baking.

Because of the pandemic, we have not been able to go camping over the last two years. As we have ten acres of land, we have decided to have a summer camp on our own land, on the far side of a mountain. Our focus in 2022 was Mongolian culture.

Thanks to the generosity of a local family with flour mills, we have set up a bakery at the Lotus Centre. We are given as much flour as we need to bake bread for our own use. Until Covid-19 struck, Paul Wilderbeek, a master baker from Brisbane, came over every year, as did a patisserie cook, to train the kids. Some of those they taught have gone on to find jobs as chefs and patisserie cooks. It's important for the kids to have as many skills as possible because they don't have extended family contacts in looking for work and a place to live – a big factor for young people in Mongolia. It makes life harder for my children. They stay at Lotus until they can manage independently.

The largest number of babies and children we've had at Lotus at any one time is 150. We currently have eighty. Eight of our teenage boys and girls have started at university this year in Ulaanbaatar. One of the first to go to university was actually left in my yard one night when she was a baby. She is the daughter of one of the street kids who had a hard life and was caught up in domestic violence, prostitution and selling alcohol.

I have sixteen staff, mostly paid. Bolormaa, a local woman, took on a paid position at Lotus when she was eighteen. Now in her late thirties, she is still working with me. She managed the Lotus Centre in 2021 while I went to visit my elderly mother in New South Wales and couldn't get back to Mongolia for months because of the pandemic.

TURNING POINTS

The hardest part of life at the Lotus Centre is meeting the running costs – paying the wages, buying food and clothes, paying bills. I love being with the children and find the administrative side of raising money difficult. My Taiwanese friends were generous in the early years of Lotus, but I no longer go regularly to Taiwan to raise money. We now rely entirely on donations from individuals and businesses, both in Mongolia and overseas. A UK lawyer, Fraser McColl, came as a volunteer then set up a Lotus Foundation charity in the United Kingdom, which brings us in a valuable regular income. We also get donations from Australia, mainly thanks to Diana Carlton in Melbourne, who came and worked with us as a volunteer for four months in 2000. Overseas visitors to the centre often give us donations.

Recently, as Mongolia has become richer, we are attracting contributions from local businesses. Over the past few years, the number of wealthy people in Ulaanbaatar has grown as the economy has picked up. When I first arrived, there were only 300 cars in the country. Now there are thousands. It's the same with telephones: you had to wait five or six years to get a phone and hardly anybody had one, which made Mongolia even more isolated from the rest of the world. I managed to get a phone by paying something under the table. People would come to me to use it. Now, of course, everyone has a mobile – often second-hand.

When I became a nun, I made a commitment to work wherever I was sent. After establishing the Lotus Centre, I worried that Ānanda Mārga would move me on at some point. So, over time, I gradually withdrew from the organisation. The thousands of children who have lived at the Lotus Centre have all been loved and cared for and given life skills. My commitment now is to them.

'I see myself as a public spokesperson for lost souls, for the ignorant, for those wanting to know more.'

Jack Charles

Finding the wisdom of the Elders

For me, the big epiphany happened the last time I was in jail. It was 2005 and my twenty-second time in the nick. People in the jail called me 'Unc' and gave me that semblance of respect, I suppose, because of my high profile as an actor. I was given respect by both the criminals and the workers there. Not long before finishing my sentence I undertook the month-long Marumali Journey of Healing program, delivered by Aunty Lorraine Peeters and her daughter Shaan Hamann.[12] It was really in-depth work. Marumali changed my life forever – it was my turning point. It set me on the path of self-discovery, on the 'who the fuck do I think I am' journey.

The program gave me time for some deep personal introspection. In Loddon Prison you got seventeen hours alone in your slot, so when the Marumali Program finished for the day I used to turn the telly down in my cell, lie back and just reflect on where I'd been, who I was and the lost opportunities. The shift within me was powerful.

I was four months old when I was taken from my mother, the oldest of eleven kids she lost, thanks to Australia's shameful assimilation policy. I was placed in the Melbourne City Mission Home in Brunswick for two years, then sent to the Box Hill Boys' Home, run by the Salvation Army. There were 200 of us. I was the only Aboriginal kid there. It was a place of beatings and serious sexual abuse. He [the abuser] came to my bed first and mucked about with me, but we were all vulnerable. Everybody in that dorm was vulnerable. It's a memory that kept on sprouting new avenues, new memories, every time I saw the articles about what was happening with the Catholics.

So many of us were not raised by our family. We were tossed around from institution to institution and ended up naturally in that prison situation and becoming serious dedicated recidivists. What we had been missing was a heritage to look back on, and family, and community. Being a stolen person means you're always trying to find out who the hell you are. Marumali opened up a space for grief and trauma, healing and connection. It was incredibly hard work.

The Royal Commission into Institutional Responses to Child Sexual Abuse was going on at the time I was serving that last jail sentence and I ran into this group of fellows from the Boys' Home. We were all collecting our methadone from the prison doctor and they came up to me and said, 'Jack Charles, do you remember us?' I didn't actually remember them, but they remembered me. They asked for my phone number so that when I was released they could give it to Ryan Carlisle Thomas, the class-action legal mob.

They said, 'We reckon you're the best person to validate and give credence to the stories of what went on there.' And I did get a call within a week of returning home (this was the first time I had a home to go to on leaving prison). Giving that evidence at the royal commission kept me stable and focused on the work I had done with the Marumali Program. I found it amazing that I was totally believed by the people questioning me. Eventually, in 2008, we got money from the Salvos. I gave most of it away that Christmas to people struggling in the flats and on the streets of Fitzroy and Collingwood. Everybody around here got a chop because it was blood money. All I bought myself was an electric scooter.

I was fourteen when I left the Salvos and was placed with a foster family in Blackburn, the Murphys, and went straight to work as an apprentice glass beveller. I was good at it and learned to love it. After a couple of years I was cajoled by the boys at work to go to Collingwood and Fitzroy. 'There's a lot of blackfellas over there, Jack,' they said. 'Bet you've got family among them.' So, one Thursday night, with a full pay packet that I'd normally hand over to my foster mum, I took a tram to Brunswick Street, Fitzroy, and jumped off at Gertrude Street. Within minutes an old blackfella grabbed me and yelled, 'You're Blanchie Charles's boy!' He ushered me over to the Builders Arms. Nearly every face there was black. I'd entered another world. It was 1960: I was nearly seventeen and finding family for the first time.

I got back late that night to Mrs Murphy's and said, 'Joy oh joy, I just found Mum! She's still alive! She lives in Swan Hill.' Mrs Murphy had always told me I was an orphan and I thought she'd be pleased. But she was angry and after a furious argument I went to bed. No sooner had I put on my pyjamas than she called me to the front door. There was a police divvy wagon outside and I was thrown in. I was shocked and frightened. We drove for ages to a place called Turana, a youth detention centre in Parkville. I cried myself to sleep. Nobody told me that what I had done in not asking Mrs Murphy's permission to contact Mum was illegal under the assimilation policy. That's how my life of crime started.

The next morning, I saw all these other failed adopted kids, fostered kids, some of them black. We had all failed and that was a criminal offence. For us black kids, actually our first criminal offence was being taken. My first criminal record stated, 'Jack Charles, four months old

Aboriginal child in need of care and attention.' That was an offence in those days. Premier Daniel Andrews' government expunged those criminal records in the middle of 2018. He's even admitted that the Stolen Generation was a form of genocide.

In 2001, I was approached by Amiel Courtin-Wilson about doing a film on my life. He called it *Bastardy*. It took seven years; two of them I was doing one-year jail sentences. If it wasn't for Amiel I don't think I would be alive today. Like the Marumali program, *Bastardy* changed the course of my life. I didn't hide anything – my alcohol addiction, drug addiction, burglaries, prison sentences. I even outed myself, which I hadn't intended to do, but once I'm stoned with a camera in front of me, I unleash.

Actually, I unleash whether I'm stoned or not. I put it all out there and I was happy Amiel included the more confronting elements of my journey, like the self-injecting, the sleeping rough. People who are struggling with their own addictions see themselves in my story. Many of them know me; many of them shared a needle with me. I got off the heroin with the help of the Victorian Aboriginal Health Service. The doctor there put me on to Turning Point in Gertrude Street.[13]

Bastardy premiered twice at the Melbourne International Film Festival in 2008. People were lined up, wrapped around the building – evidence of the fact that Melburnians wanted to see the actor who's down on hard times because of heavy addiction to drugs and doing jail time occasionally. All my former comrades from Box Hill came, the ones who were still alive. Retired chief inspectors, whom I'd led on many a merry chase over the years, came, and some working police. Even people who I'd robbed on the other side of the Yarra, ironically on my mum's land, Bunurong Country, came. I justified robbing them by saying they're paying rent on Mum's land. I couldn't have taken that to a magistrate. I would have been given another five years and told to snap out of it.

I realise that with *Bastardy* people got to understand just one Stolen person's journey, one person's struggle. And I was well known as a busker, actor and cat burglar because I was headline news as a serial pest, a nuisance. It never shamed me because that was my life in those days. With the film, Amiel didn't take advantage of me. I took advantage of him because he couldn't get a shot out of me unless I conned $50 out of him so I could go up to the Napier Street flats to the dealer.

Amiel's film opened up my life. There were many people wanting to hear more of my story and people who knew me well who were absolutely thrilled to the core that I had put myself in the eye of the Australian community. I said that from that first premiere night with this documentary I could be taken seriously by the government. I proclaimed myself an Elder, a local Kadaitcha man.[14] An Elder is somebody who is working behind the scenes, in front of the scenes and being an advocate for his community. And in being an advocate for the community, you're also impacting on the communities around the nation, because word gets around.

Doing film festivals around the nation gave me a great public forum. In 2009, Amiel submitted *Bastardy* to the Sheffield International Documentary Film Festival, the place to showcase docos in the United Kingdom. They wanted me over there for two Q&As, so I went and got a passport. No problem. But the British High Commission knocked me back. I'd forgotten that I had a criminal record. I screamed down the phone at Amiel, 'They fucking knocked me back!' Missy Higgins was on the other end of the line too, and she got on to so many people in the arts I was given a waiver.

TURNING POINTS

Working on the doco and doing the Marumali program gave me the strength to get off the methadone. It's a bastard of a drug. The Germans invented it during the war to use instead of morphine. It's an insidious drug to come off. I've seen people jumping back on heroin to get off methadone. It's a vicious cycle. But I did it because I felt I had to be the real deal, the man beyond reproach, and to be seen as beyond reproach.

It was time for me to take myself seriously. I realised that once I jumped off the methadone I could perform on stage without any enhancements of any sort. I could show the rest of the community – those in the arts and in my own community – that there I was, this particular little black duck performing on stage with no heroin or methadone enhancements.

I have so much to do that I need to maintain myself in good spirits. I am lacking in lung power, but it hasn't stopped me from getting up and talking at length on any subject that I've needed to waffle on about. So I'm really pleased that I've taken myself seriously enough in hand that I am the walking, talking, definitive role model. I even did a series of courses for Elders. I'd get to meet others and get a heads-up on what they were striving for, developing their own sense of becoming elder statesmen and leaders in their own communities. It was a great opportunity to hear the stories of other individuals from around the nation.

One day I had a private word with somebody who was going to the local casino and coming back pissed. I told him to stay away, that he was an embarrassment to himself and to us. We didn't know each other but he took my word for it mainly because I had more grey hair than him. That's an element in Indigenous culture. If you've got grey hair and you're being an advocate, people listen to you.

84

Part of my purpose is to help Aboriginal inmates. My criminal record stopped me from being allowed to go back into prison to help others. That changed through my connection with the Archie Roach Foundation.[15] I have been able to go to jails and into youth detention centres, often together with Archie, to reach out to the hearts and minds of those struggling behind bars. It's my duty as an Elder. I'm a special roving ambassador for the foundation and a member of the foundation's Council of Elders.

I have an inner urge to share the journey. It's an Indigenous thing. That's why I wrote *Jack Charles: Born-again Blakfella (2019)*. A teacher took my book to the Malmsbury Youth Training Centre and had the kids take it in turns to read the book aloud. African-Australian kids, gangster kids, white Australian kids, Aboriginal kids – they were reading my book aloud. She rang up and said, 'Jack, as they're reading it some of the kids are coming up to me and saying they see elements of their own lives unfolding in your story.' She asked me to Zoom in with them the next day for a Q&A session, which I did. It was wonderful. The kids were really champing at the bit to throw questions at me. They were thrilled that I had written the book. So I said to them, 'You talk the teacher into asking the management at Malmsbury if you can see the documentary *Bastardy*,' and the management agreed. I told them that for three-quarters of that movie I was stoned. You could see how weak I was against the pulling power of the white powder. And for the last part you see the beginning of me changing. I'd just been released from prison and about to come off the methadone. By the time the film was premiered, I was an absolute cleanskin.

I believe *Bastardy* should go into every school. It's up there at the Moreland Hall Drug and Alcohol Centre in Coburg, it's well travelled.

TURNING POINTS

It's even been shown in churches. It's toured all over and boosts and empowers me because people know me wherever I go.

The fact is, I took myself in hand. I'm over sixty. I should be playing the role of an Elder statesman and that requires being up front, out front and forthright, being genuine, being beyond reproach, being true to myself and true to the community and very sensitive to the struggles that the stragglers face on a daily basis. I'm there for them. I give a lot of the fellows who come out of prison and youth detention centres a chop-out financially in my own right. That's part of my role as an Elder, to grease the palm as it were and to convince them not to use it on the dreaded shit.

I help kids reflect on their past, too. This is the kind of journey I want them to undertake when I engage with them. I did a recording for the Smiling Mind program in NAIDOC Week in 2020.[16] It was a guided meditation to calm the savage beast lying within the hearts and minds of worrywarts. I would like to do another recording specially for youth in detention centres, and for men and women in adult prisons. I want them to plug in the headphones, turn the television down, close their eyes and listen to my dulcet tones taking them inside.

I see myself as a public spokesperson for lost souls, for the ignorant, for those wanting to know more. I take advantage of the fact that my name is Jack Charles: my initials are JC. Perhaps I am the Second Coming, brown like the original. But I take this seriously because people are wanting to take me seriously. The Marumali program gave me those wings, gave me the ability to think of myself far beyond my station, as a leading black life in my community. It helped me find my purpose.

This interview was conducted in 2020. Jack Charles passed away in September 2022 and was sent off on Country by his family with a smoking ceremony.

'When opportunities have come my way,
I have been happy to take risks – sometimes a mistake,
but often it's been worthwhile.'

Gillian Triggs

Seeking social justice grounded in
international law

I wanted to work for greater social justice from an early age. Having confidence has been a key ingredient in achieving that goal. Not everybody likes outspoken young girls but, even as a teenager, I was quite confident, possibly to the irritation of others! When opportunities have come my way, I have been happy to take risks – sometimes a mistake, but often it's been worthwhile.

I do believe that good fortune is an essential element, particularly good health. Of course, I've had my share of bad luck, so I think in the end it's about mental resilience, determination and a willingness to seize opportunities. I sometimes notice that women, even young ones who have so much in front of them, can be modest, even passive, in accepting a male point of view, whereas I have been rather less inclined to do so.

My good health is genetic. My willingness to stand up for myself reflects my mother's strength. She was not particularly well educated by today's standards. She knew she was an intelligent woman but couldn't move forward without formal qualifications. She pretty much ran the business side of my father's clockmaking, watchmaking and jewellery business, so she had a vital role, but I think she was frustrated. That's why she wanted her daughters to be well educated

TURNING POINTS

and to be able to speak up for themselves. She was an enormously important influence on me.

My parents were both seventeen or so when they met in 1940, volunteering for the civil ambulance service during the Blitz in London. My father then joined the army and became a British military tank commander serving in North Africa, and my mother joined the Women's Royal Naval Service. They married in 1944 and bought a house in the North London suburb of Muswell Hill. I was born in 1945, the year the war ended.

I remember as a child being aware of European refugees on the streets of London. They were often standing on corners selling cigarettes and matches. Most of them were homeless, jobless and unable to speak English. My parents often talked about freedom, non-discrimination and racial equality as the values for which 'their' war had been fought. My sense of social justice comes from their unwavering commitment to these principles.

We migrated to Melbourne in 1958. My parents didn't think post-war London was a good place to bring up children. We settled in Croydon. A few days after we arrived, I remember sitting with neighbours watching dancers on Channel Seven and being rather critical. I had been a ballet student in London. A friend took me to one side and told me that if I kept that up, I would never adjust to life in Australia. I realised she was right: that if I was negative, I wouldn't be happy here. It was the best lesson I've ever learned.

My parents successfully re-established their business, and my younger sister, Carol, and I gained places at University High, an elite state school in Parkville where it was taken for granted that all students would go to the nearby university. The round trip from Croydon by bike, train and tram took three hours. It was hard but we loved school and wouldn't miss a day.

I enrolled at the law school at the University of Melbourne in 1964 and was one of a small group of women among 310 law students. We had brilliant teachers, but it wasn't until I attended a lecture on international law in my third year that I found my passion. The lecture was given by Dr Hans Leyser, who had come to Melbourne in the 1930s, escaping the Holocaust. He talked about the Covenant of the League of Nations, drafted in 1919, which failed to prevent World War II; the signing of the Charter of the United Nations by fifty-one countries in 1945; and the adoption of the Universal Declaration of Human Rights by the United Nations General Assembly in 1948. I walked out of that lecture fizzing with a new sense of purpose. The idea of the international rule of law has inspired and informed my professional life ever since.

The first couple of decades after university were taken up with getting married, having three children and teaching at the university, which provided the foundational skills that I have since used in so many ways. I realised that if I could speak up with some clarity, people might listen. As opportunities came my way, I found my voice and the strength to speak up.

During my time as president of the Australian Human Rights Commission I was proud of *The Forgotten Children* report, the National Inquiry into Children in Immigration Detention, in 2014. It was disappointing that the government and part of the media rejected the factually and legally accurate findings and recommendations. Perhaps I got under their skin, but perhaps that is a measure of success. Then prime minister Tony Abbott and attorney-general George Brandis declared they had no confidence in me. I responded, 'If I were to be flattered by the government, taxpayers should demand my salary back, for I would not be doing my job.'

When we started *The Forgotten Children* report, there were 1100 children in indefinite detention. Afterwards, that number dropped to 200. Now it's zero.[17] I think our work at the commission, together with that of the faith-based and other civil society groups – including Grandmothers for Refugees (of which I am patron), human rights activists and litigation lawyers – collectively, we were able to shift public opinion. I think it is fair to say we have had some positive outcomes of the work we've all been doing to encourage Australia to meet its obligations to refugees in need of international protection.

The Australian Human Rights Commission has also generated some stimulating public discussions on human rights over the past few years. Often you need a quick slogan to capture people's attention. I find that by constantly stressing that Australia is the only country in the western world without a charter of rights is cutting through.

I am convinced that we have a serious deficit in the legal protection of human rights in Australia and that we need to consider introducing a legislated federal charter of rights. Indeed, enactment of such a law has been Labor Party policy. Had Labor won the election in 2019, I believe they would have introduced a charter of rights, perhaps in a second term. I'm inclined to think a charter has a better chance of adoption if we have bipartisan support. But, for the moment, the Coalition is reluctant to agree to a charter of any kind. It's notable that Queensland adopted a charter of rights in 2019, Victoria has had one since 2006 and the Australian Capital Territory adopted one many years ago. The challenge is to find agreement at the federal level, where we so desperately need it. All political parties should support a human rights charter, but I'm afraid the Coalition will not consider the adoption of any legislative or constitutional human rights protection.

We do not have a right of freedom of speech in our constitution and I think Australians are starting to be concerned. The power of employers and the need to protect LGBTQI people from abuse – these and other issues are prompting people to ask whether we need greater protections. There is a growing awareness in Australia that we have somehow slipped behind Europe, Canada and the United States in protecting civil liberties. Many Australians are not well informed about their constitution. Today, however, many are asking about the limits on freedom of speech. The 2019 raids on the ABC offices and on a News Corp journalist's home, for example, were concerning.[18] People are starting to examine the reasonable limits on executive powers generally.

We're fortunate to have the ABC and programs like *Four Corners*. With my colleagues, we did a report on the Don Dale Detention Centre two years before the *Four Corners* exposé, and nothing was done about it. The *Four Corners* program in 2016 brought the matter into the public light and is an example of independent investigative journalism.

In September 2019, I flew to Switzerland to take up my appointment as United Nations Assistant Secretary-General and Assistant High Commissioner with the United Nations High Commissioner for Refugees. I was seventy-four and it was hard to leave everything behind – family and friends, the dog and our house – but this chance to work on the protection of those forcibly displaced (about 84 million people globally) is a great honour for me. My UN appointment advances my work with the Australian Human Rights Commission. Perhaps United Nations colleagues read *The Forgotten Children* report and said, 'We want a straight-talking Australian.' Well, they've got one!

'What would have become of me if I'd baulked and decided not to blow the whistle?'

Andrew Wilkie

Bearing the cost of a moral compass

I was born in Tamworth, New South Wales, in 1961 to fundamentalist Catholic parents. I think they and my Catholic education helped inculcate in me a certain sense of principles and values, but on the whole it was a very conventional, don't-rock-the-boat sort of upbringing. This probably helps explain why, when I was a cadet at Duntroon, I joined the Young Liberals, although it was a very different Liberal Party under Malcolm Fraser, and as much a social club for me as anything else. I left after two years. I matured personally and probably politically over the next twenty-something years, but the key turning point was my year in Government House in Canberra in 1989.

I slept just down the corridor from Bill and Dallas Hayden, and as an ADC on his personal staff would often eat with Bill, travel with him, sit with him in the car and socialise with them both at Government House. That was a really formative year for me philosophically. I changed from being conservative, moving to the centre, even to the left. I learned about the ideas of socialism and that communities should look after their own. I also learned more about social justice and was mixing with people I had a lot of respect for. I met Gough Whitlam, I met Malcolm Fraser, I met Paul Keating and Bob Hawke – big people of the period. Major leaders. It was probably the most formative year of my life.

For the next twenty-odd years I led a full life in the army. I did a Bachelor of Arts degree at the Royal Military College, Duntroon, and graduate diplomas in Management and Defence Studies. In 1991 I married a fellow officer, Simone Burt, who became the first woman commanding officer at Duntroon. She would go on to become a major general, the highest-ranking woman in the Australian Army in the general stream to that time.

I was always up for a debate at the bar in the officers' mess. I can remember as a lieutenant advocating for gays in the military and arguing about the rights and wrongs of the Vietnam War ten years after the fall of Saigon. By the time I arrived at the Office of National Assessments (ONA) in 1999, I was probably more worldly than some Army officers, and I think I was certainly more open-minded than a lot of people.

ONA, Australia's senior intelligence agency, coordinated the nation's intelligence effort. One of the attractions of working there was that I felt I was working on the big issues. I was thinking big. Most people at ONA looked at a fairly narrow field. For instance, there was a China analyst, an Indonesia analyst, a Russia analyst, a Europe analyst. I was always in more thematic areas: military issues, transnational issues like terrorism, irregular people movements, drug running and crime.

This, crucially, gave me a broader access to intelligence material than a lot of my colleagues. If you were a China analyst, for example, you only looked at China material. As a strategic analyst in trans-national issues, I could delve into the secret material of any country. It was important work, and I felt I was making a difference. But at some point I realised that I wasn't making a difference, that while I was at ONA I was actually part of the problem – the problem being that the government was lying to the Australian people and going to take us into a war based on a lie, all those lies.

I was pretty much onside until late 2002, when we knew war was brewing. I knew I'd be involved in the work on it, as an ex-military person, and had been tracking the Iraq issue for quite some time. At the end of 2002, I was required to do a significant assessment of the possible humanitarian consequences of a war. That required me to read about the war. I wrote a report that had the highest classification you could imagine, as it drew on very sensitive material. It wasn't passing judgement on the war, but simply saying to the prime minister and relevant cabinet ministers that if we go to war you need to be mindful of the possible outcomes. Looking back now, the numbers who died were probably beyond even my worst thoughts.

Simone and I took a Christmas break in New Zealand, staying at a bed-and-breakfast where the hosts were hostile about the likelihood of Australia going to war in Iraq. I remember arguing the Australian government's case with them and thinking it was a hard argument to make. I was feeling restless and uneasy and under enormous emotional pressure over my increasing concerns about the war and I started cautiously expressing my reservations to a work colleague. My profound stress at the time put an intolerable strain on my relationship with Simone. We split just after our return – so on one level my Iraq experience cost me my marriage, though that would be to oversimplify.

I made up my mind in February 2003 that I had to do something. I contacted journalist Laurie Oakes, who warned me what happens when you blow the whistle. I had no idea. I was clueless. I did know I'd be out of a job because I was going to resign. I knew that what I would say would be very controversial, but I assumed that there would be a furore for a couple of days and then it would all die down, after which I'd get on with my life, having no idea what that would look like. I had my army pension. I'd be a free agent, though I did have a concern that I might be locked up. I put my affairs in order, paid my bills and gave a spare key to my apartment to my friend and colleague Kate Burton, in case she needed to get in and clear it out.

I don't think I ever kidded myself that I was going to stop the war, not least because the Americans were going to war regardless of Australia. But I was prepared to go to jail to get my message out: that there were virtually no weapons of mass destruction, there were no links with al-Qaeda, that the real reason for Australia being a part of the invasion of Iraq was our subservience to the United States and John Howard's personal relationship with George W. Bush. A lot came down to the United States promoting and safeguarding its global authority. Also, there was a Congressional midterm election, and in early 2002 the Republicans weren't going very well, so they really whipped up the Iraq threat. They needed a Falklands and made Saddam Hussein the bogeyman. I think there was a personal thing with George W. Bush finishing the job his father started. And oil was in the mix as well, but it wasn't an oil war. That was a second-level thing.

The news broke on the evening of 11 March – the day I resigned. The Australian government moved quickly to discredit me. Kim Jones, the Director-General of ONA, held a press conference at Parliament House saying I knew little about Iraq, that I had no idea what I was talking about. The next day the prime minister's media people were at the press gallery telling them that I was unhinged, that I was having an emotional breakdown because of my split with Simone. The actual story was that I was so troubled by the government's misconduct, it was the final straw in my marriage.

Although suddenly every journalist in the country and overseas wanted to talk to me, on a personal level I was completely and utterly isolated, especially in Canberra. I instantly lost a lot of friends, who were horrified at my behaviour. I dumped some friends for their own protection and dumped others because of what I learnt about them through this whole process.

It was very hard initially, but I knew I was right. I just had to get through it. It wasn't an option to curl up in a foetal position. I had my reputation and integrity to protect. I had to sound confident about my message, otherwise people wouldn't believe me. It would have discredited me, discredited my story and backed up the government's false claim that I was a wreck.

It took a while for my allegations to be shown to be true. After about six weeks, people in the media started to query, well, where are the weapons of mass destruction?

You lose a lot of skin going through this sort of thing. I find that even now I can get quite emotional. My story has ended remarkably well, but at a cost. It's taken its toll and I think I am wounded emotionally. I'm very respectful of the average Australian whistleblower who doesn't get the happy ending. It's harder now for security officials than when I blew the whistle. We have in this country what I characterise as legalised corruption. It's appalling. We need meaningful whistleblower protection, including for security officials; we need a federal integrity commission with teeth; we need a bill of rights; we need political donation reform; and we need effective laws to protect media freedoms.

Something I've reflected on deeply is what would have become of me if I hadn't spoken out. Having assessed that the government was lying and taking us into an unjust war, what would have become of me if I'd baulked and decided not to blow the whistle? I will never

TURNING POINTS

know the answer, but put yourself in my shoes. What if, after months of heartache and research and wrestling with my conscience and deciding the government was dishonest, that this was an unjust war, I had decided to keep my mouth shut and then my assessment was proven correct and countless people died? I don't think I would have been able to live with myself. I'm not a suicidal man, but that probably would've been enough. Knowing what I knew, I wouldn't have been able to live with the knowledge that I hadn't had the strength to speak out. So this was what compelled me.

'In Ethiopia, I expected that by filling my days with helping others, I would gain spiritual fullness and a reprieve from my relentless questioning about how to live a meaningful life.'

Julie Sprigg

Employing the healing power of physiotherapy

I decided to study physiotherapy when I was in Year 12, after flicking through a careers booklet and reading that physiotherapy skills were sorely needed in developing countries. That was the clincher for me. Throughout my studies I always planned to work somewhere overseas one day, a place where I thought I might make a difference.

I'd been taught by nuns at Catholic schools and, seeing the sisters' dedication, was attracted to the idea of having a calling to do something meaningful with my life. That feeling persisted after I graduated from university. I desired deeper fulfilment than working nine to five just to pay off a mortgage or accumulate possessions. I became increasingly aware of the injustice that asylum seekers face and became heavily involved in political activism. This drive to find meaning in my life intensified until it was all-consuming.

Physiotherapy is about rehabilitation, about regaining and maximising movement; it is a mix of human biology and psychology. I was twenty-eight and working as a physiotherapist in Western Australia when I met Sister Maeve, a nun who had spent twenty years working in Africa. We both volunteered with asylum seekers at the detention centre in Port Hedland and spent a lot of time talking about social justice. When Sister Maeve suggested I might like to work with her

TURNING POINTS

order of sisters in Ethiopia for a few months, I jumped at the chance. The sisters there, she told me, ran a clinic for people with disabilities in the capital, Addis Ababa, and were looking for a physio. Sister Maeve said, 'Be prepared, though – the poverty and sickness will be like nothing you've ever seen. You will never be the same again.'

Sister Maeve was right. My decision to go to Ethiopia was a turning point in how I understood the world, and the choices I made to find some peace with my place in it. I flew to Ethiopia in October 2004. The sisters' clinic in Addis Ababa was a converted shipping container with a door and window cut into its metal walls. It was just big enough to fit a desk, a low plinth, a bench and a floor mat. The physio equipment was crammed into any remaining spaces. In the time I worked there I saw a full range of patients, from babies to the elderly, many with diagnoses I had never encountered before.

My first patient was Ammanuel, who was four years old but looked eighteen months. He lived with cerebral palsy and was unable to speak. He had very little movement. His mum carried him everywhere tied to her back. She couldn't find work because of the stigma of his disability, and they were regularly evicted because she couldn't pay the rent – the equivalent of about AU$3.50 a month. Part of the physio focus was helping Ammanuel sit independently so his mother could do some work.

The sisters linked Ammanuel's mother into the onsite community-based rehabilitation program, which included livelihoods for people with disabilities. The program empowered her to set up a microbusiness. She used her start-up capital loan to purchase a charcoal burner, a jug and some other implements and started selling injera – traditional Ethiopian bread – by the roadside. With the income from her stall, she could pay rent and feed the two of them as well as buy a second set of clothes. This was the first time I saw how physiotherapy could be part of a plan to help a family gain economic independence and turn their lives around.

During the three months I lived and worked with the sisters in Addis Ababa, I became friends with Sister Almaz, who was in the capital to collect supplies for her programs in Welega, a remote area close to the Ethiopia–Sudan border. The sisters there ran a school and were raising funds to start a support program for women. Sister Almaz invited me to work with them as they had so many families with children with disabilities, but no local services. She was very interested in the rehabilitation training I had devised for the clinic in Addis Ababa and was keen for me to train her staff.

While working in the rural clinic with Sister Almaz, I saw many kids with delayed development due to severe malnutrition. Sister Almaz explained that in addition to food shortages, the malnutrition was compounded by a lack of protein and lack of a varied diet. Mothers were feeding their children corn, the only food given by aid agencies. Before the famines of the 1980s, mothers had access to a variety of food sources. However, the aid agencies that arrived during the famines only gave out corn. This continued in the decades to follow, and families became dependent on corn and lost the knowledge of how to grow some of their nutritious traditional foods, such as bananas and tomatoes.

This was a real eye-opener for me, and through discussions with Sister Almaz I started to see the effects of prolonged aid that only focused on immediate needs. Her programs demonstrated a better way of supporting people in extreme poverty. They met an immediate need with an eye to long-term practical support, such as women's livelihoods. The dependency I saw in Welega was a legacy issue, the result of decades of aid. These days there are stringent rules demanding

TURNING POINTS

that aid (now called development assistance) should be sustainable and meet long-term outcomes. The focus is on change rather than charity.

Although I loved working with Sister Almaz, I was very aware of the short-term nature of my input into her programs in Welega and the even more remote outlying districts we visited. Patients and their families were eager for help, and while I could show them exercises, it was distressing to see people with chronic problems and severe functional limitations with no chance of a follow-up. One session with a physio and suggestions for exercises wouldn't have much impact in the long term. I wished there was a community-based rehabilitation program or a physio clinic I could refer them to, but there were no services available for thousands of kilometres.

When I arrived in Ethiopia, there were only seven Ethiopian physiotherapists, most of them trained outside the country. While working in Welega I heard there was a physiotherapy degree course at the University of Gondar, a former imperial city. Sister Almaz urged me to call and see if I might work with them. To my amazement I was invited to join the staff of the physiotherapy department to teach classes and supervise students on the wards of the university hospital. I was sad to leave Sister Almaz. She was so much fun to be with, as well as having such a profound influence on how I understood social justice. But I was excited to start the next part of my adventure.

Up until now I had been somewhat professionally isolated. There was no more-experienced physio to call on with difficult cases, so I was delighted when I got to the hospital at Gondar and became part of a team of eight other expat physiotherapists and three Ethiopian assistants. Being a university hospital, the cases were often acute and confronting, but the team was skilled at dealing with conditions that were completely new to me.

106

Most days my caseload included the new admission of a child paralysed from the waist down due to tuberculosis of the spine. At first, I had no idea how to prepare a treatment plan – I had never seen a patient with TB before. It uncommon in Australia except for rare occurrences in remote Aboriginal communities, where it is usually treated in the lungs before it has a chance to spread.

One of the many children I saw with TB was eight-year-old Samira. I supervised the physiotherapy students' assessment and treatment for her, and we worked with her over three months. During this time she went from having no movement in her legs to being strong enough to stand and take a step with a walking frame.

Samira's mum then had to make the hard decision about staying in Gondar for her daughter's rehab or taking her back to their distant village so that she could make sure her other children were fed and safe. When she chose to leave, I was devastated. But to our surprise and delight, when they came back for a three-month check, Samira was able to walk into the clinic. Her mum had ensured that she did her physio exercises daily at home. Being able to walk again meant Samira could go back to school, play with her friends in the fields and have a life trajectory like her peers. It was a great feeling to have contributed to her recovery from TB.

Another complicated case was that of nine-year-old Sara. When she was admitted, she was unable to walk due to a stroke. She had TB in the chest, lymph nodes, spleen and liver, as well as heart failure. Her father carried her from the ward to the physio room every morning and afternoon. Despite her huge health challenges, she made a great recovery after three months of medical treatment and twice-daily physiotherapy with the students. She lived in a remote village with no vehicle access, so we dropped her off with her dad at the road closest to her village. She gave us a huge grin and a wave and walked on home.

It was such rewarding work to see my paediatric patients thrive, despite the structural inequalities that led to them having diseases that are largely eliminated in most richer countries. The physiotherapy students were learning new skills every day and getting closer to graduation, and I was really enjoying my job.

There were times, however, when the lack of resources was very challenging. Families often came in from extremely remote villages with kids who had complex and multiple disabilities. Sometimes parents, having heard about the new physiotherapy program, travelled for days to bring their children to the hospital, only to find physiotherapy could provide limited support. If these kids had been in Australia, they would have had a multidisciplinary team, specialised education and communication support – perhaps even motorised wheelchairs and other equipment. But in Gondar we were limited to providing hands-on physiotherapy and perhaps a link to a community-based rehabilitation program with grassroots workers, though only three such programs ran in very small areas. In those situations, I found it difficult to tell a family that we couldn't do anything for them.

The challenges in my workplace were compounded by the wider political situation. I had done a lot of background reading on Ethiopia's history, so I knew it had recently emerged from a long period of repression. But there was no way that I could comprehend in advance what it means to live in that situation. While I was in Gondar there was an election, the first democratic election in Ethiopia since the previous dictatorship had ended. Days, weeks and then months passed, and still no results were announced. We heard that students in Addis Ababa were demonstrating about what they claimed was a rigged election.

There were rumours of violent clashes with the police, of hundreds of arrests, of dozens of deaths.

Then the unrest came to Gondar and spread across the country. Demonstrators and opposition leaders were put under house arrest or jailed without charge, and people were shot in the streets during protests. I only understood repression on an abstract level, having spent time with asylum seekers in Australia who'd come from Iran, Afghanistan and the Democratic Republic of Congo. Their firsthand accounts of what it was like to live under a repressive regime meant that at first I wasn't shocked by the conflict or the political uprising. I knew how lucky we were in Australia to have peaceful democratic processes. What surprised me was how personal the repression became. I lay awake in bed hearing gunfire in the streets, not knowing who was getting hurt. There were fires in the dormitories and I thought my students were being shot. Then, when our university course was threatened and it looked like all our hard work might be overturned by the political situation, I was blindsided.

I had raced off to have this adventure, to 'do good', because of my connection to Sister Maeve and so was completely unprepared for dealing with conflict. My expat colleagues were placed with aid organisations and had preparatory training. If I had done the same I might have had guidance for culture shock and strategies to help me cope emotionally. That lack of preparedness made me much more vulnerable. I turned to journalling as a way of processing my feelings. I came home from work, wrote; set my alarm for 4.30 am, wrote. I had so much going on in my head that I often wrote a thousand words a day.

When I arrived in Ethiopia, I expected that by filling my days with helping others, I would gain spiritual fullness and a reprieve from my relentless questioning about how to live a meaningful life. Now I just had new questions. My long journal entries eventually became the basis for a manuscript I took nine years to complete. *Small Steps: A Physio in Ethiopia* was published in 2020. Had I not kept a journal, I could never have written my book, describing and reflecting on my experiences.

The civil unrest eased, but as it got closer to the time for the students' graduation, bureaucratic issues at the university jeopardised the physiotherapy degree. Although I loved my work and found it rewarding, I found the frustrations begin to outweigh the rewards. I started to feel angry at the university administration, and at a government system that paid its staff so poorly they couldn't care properly for seriously ill kids. I couldn't see beyond the structural inequalities that manifested in day-to-day hygiene and safety issues. There were not enough medicines nor enough water for basic hygiene, like washing hands, mopping floors or cleaning sheets.

Because I had no preparation, I didn't know how to separate myself from the situation and my mental health started to decline. I later learned the various terms for this, such as 'vicarious trauma' and 'compassion fatigue', but at the time all I felt was anger and sadness at so much needless suffering. After two years I returned to Australia heartbroken at giving up my dream career. It wasn't until much later that I realised I hadn't lost faith in my work or my love for it. It was just that I was exhausted.

If I was giving advice to my younger self, I would say: make sure you have the right support to guard against crashing and burning and feeling that gaping sense of despair because the dream doesn't match the reality. If you want to make a long-term commitment to this work, get mental health support, perhaps counselling, and take breaks rather than giving it absolutely everything and then ending up completely depleted.

On my return to Australia in 2006, I struggled to slot back into my old life. Things improved when I took up a position as a project officer with the international development organisation CBM Australia. My new colleagues had had similar experiences to mine and understood the challenges of working in developing countries. Most of them had good professional support and were able to maintain some personal distance from their work, which I strived to do also.

I owe most of my spiritual recovery to joining an unconventional church. We met in a café once a week and discussed the meaning of life, moral philosophy and the search for purpose. This meant I was eventually able to reframe my experiences in Ethiopia to be about resilience and hope, joy and friendship.

The physiotherapy profession in Ethiopia has changed dramatically in the years since I lived there, and the political situation was more stable by the time I wrote my book. There are about 700 physiotherapists now, widely dispersed, with physio clinics in all the major government-run hospitals and the big regional towns. There has been a revolution in the way physios can support community-based rehab programs. There have also been shifts in the way that disability is understood, with significantly less discrimination and stigma in the community.

I was grateful when former students of mine approached me, among others, for support and resources when they set up the Ethiopian Physiotherapists' Association. Many of my past students have gone on to do their master's in physiotherapy internationally. Some have emailed to ask for a reference, surprising and delighting me with comments like 'I've never forgotten you as my teacher' and 'You were so meaningful, you meant so much to me.' These words are so validating to read after such despair. I am grateful I had the opportunity to contribute to systemic change.

TURNING POINTS

Part of my motivation for writing *Small Steps* so many years after working in Ethiopia is that the stories of the children never left me. But I also wanted to capture the roller-coaster of youthful idealism and the painful life lesson that there are no simple solutions to complex problems. I am glad my book has sparked discussions about global inequalities and the role each of us can play to alleviate them.

'When I get older, I don't want my son or my grandkids to ask me why I didn't do anything – or why I didn't do more.'

Inala Cooper

Using her voice for the Indigenous community

It's important to tell the stories of our Elders and of our ancestors. This tradition of storytelling in our culture keeps it alive.

I feel very close to my grandmother, Patricia Djiagween, even though I never met her. She died in 1960, before I was born. In my book *Marrul: Aboriginal Identity and the Fight for Rights* (2022), I describe her as being beautiful and staunch. There are some photos of her, thankfully, and she looks beautiful. People in the family describe her as beautiful inside and out. I see her as staunch because she fought for her human rights and was determined to keep her family together. She was from Broome, where she had two daughters from a relationship with Abu Kassim bin Marah, a Malaysian man. She and my aunties were sent away, first to the Beagle Bay Mission, and later to Christmas Creek, where she met my grandfather, John Dodson, who was always known as Snowy.

Snowy and Patricia wanted to get married and settle down together, but the state of Western Australia wouldn't allow it. Snowy's background is a bit of a mystery, but he must have passed as white because he was charged with cohabiting with a native woman, which was a breach of the law. He was put in Fremantle Prison for eighteen months. Eventually he was released and made his way back up north to find my grandmother. They were given permission to marry in 1947 on condition that they left the state, which they did. They settled in Katherine in the Northern Territory.

I have gained an understanding of the type of woman Patricia was from people who remember her, people who have spoken about her character and qualities. My dad, Mick Dodson, and my uncles and aunties were strongly influenced by her, and I am too. I am told I am like her. I feel she is within me, that our spirits are linked.

Dad was the first Aboriginal to graduate from law in Australia. He became a barrister and human rights activist. His brother, Uncle Pat, entered politics and became a Labor senator in Western Australia. They are both strong Aboriginal leaders. I am proud of all aspects of my identity. They have made me who I am. I am an Aboriginal person first and foremost, but also a person with Irish and German heritage too. Mum and Mum's side of the family did an incredible job in ensuring that my brother and I were secure in our identities, and that included being proud of being Aboriginal and of the work that Dad and Uncle Pat were doing.

I grew up in Port Fairy, in Victoria, but spent my early years on a farm in Codrington, about twenty-five kilometres away. Being a country girl has also had an impact on my view of the world. Life was very different then, in the 1980s and 1990s. We didn't have the internet, so everything was happening in real time. If you missed the news, you missed it. If you didn't get the paper that day, you couldn't just look it up online; you had to find the actual copy. There were many days when Dad and Uncle Pat were in the public eye and I would hear about it from the teachers at school, who would say, 'We heard your dad on the radio' or 'We saw your dad on TV'.

Much of my understanding of what Dad was doing came through seeing him on television. He would rarely talk about work on phone calls home or on family holidays. That was fun time. But as I grew older I saw him working really hard for the things that mattered to him. I saw a person striving for social justice within our Aboriginal and Torres Strait Islander communities and the broader society. I was also aware of Dad's work on the National Inquiry into the Separation of Aboriginal and Torres Strait Islander Children from Their Families that resulted in the *Bringing Them Home* report in 1997.

The work Dad and Uncle Pat did on the Royal Commission into Aboriginal Deaths in Custody was massive. I was a teenager when that was happening. When the report came out in 1991, Dad sent us copies. There were over 300 recommendations and I remember thinking, *Something's going to change.* But it hasn't. In many cases, things have gotten worse. There have been over 500 recorded deaths in custody since the royal commission handed down its report, and the failure is that governments have not accepted or implemented the recommendations.

The same can be said for the removal of children from their families. That still happens at an alarmingly high rate. The other injustice that is inflicted on our kids is the huge incarceration rates, particularly in the Northern Territory. So there's still a lot that needs doing. We can't ignore the work that's already been done by Elders in the past, but sadly it speaks to how racist our country is when so much time and energy and expertise is put into providing recommendations on how to make things better, on how to have justice for First Nations peoples, and nothing changes.

I believe people who are not Aboriginal and Torres Strait Islanders must have the courage to support the need for social justice – our leaders especially, from the prime minister all the way down. They need to make change and create appropriate policies together with us. It's very easy to be a coward and hide behind politics instead of stepping up and doing the right thing. Politics is a dirty game. It seems to me that if you don't have the fortitude to rise above it and actually do what's right, you shouldn't hold power.

I used to be hopeful. I saw hope as a form of resistance, but my feelings on this have changed. I'm not without hope, but I was stirred when I read Chelsea Watego's book *Another Day in the Colony* (2021). She has strong views on hope, claiming we don't need to be hopeful, that we as First Nations peoples need to be sovereign. That really spoke to me. Our sovereignty is our strength and that's all we need to focus on.

Two turning points in my life led me to feel passionately about social justice. One was when I was fifteen and went to the United Nations in Geneva with Dad. He was part of what was called the Working Group on Indigenous Populations. This was a massive moment for me in terms of understanding what self-determination is, and better understanding what the Universal Declaration of Human Rights is and why there needed to be a particular Declaration on the Rights of Indigenous Peoples. It was such a privilege to go to Geneva and see what the United Nations was and how it worked. I knew then that I would have some purpose in life relating to human rights.

At the same time, I aspired to be involved in the performing arts. Mum and Dad encouraged me in this. I wanted to dance and act and did a Bachelor of Arts in Drama and Contemporary Dance. I worked in the arts for some time, then in the public service, but everything changed when I went with Dad to the United Nations in New York in about 2010. That was Dad's final year in his role as an expert member for Australia of the United Nations Permanent Forum on Indigenous Issues. I wanted to go while Dad was still part of it and paid my own way, taking annual leave from my job. Dad asked me to be his assistant, which was terrific, as I got to sit behind him each day for two weeks in the General Assembly and go to closed meetings. The work involved summarising papers, preparing correspondence to other members and fetching whatever Dad needed. It was a wonderful way to be involved and see the inner workings.

This experience solidified for me what I wanted to do with my life. I enrolled in a Master of Human Rights Law and embarked on a career that involved social justice. I felt called to work to make education more accessible to Aboriginal and Torres Strait Islander peoples, and that includes ensuring that universities are environments where our mob feel they belong. Much of my work over the past few years has focused on this, including my current role as director of Murrup Barak, the Melbourne Institute of Indigenous Development at the University of Melbourne. Murrup is a Woiwurrung word meaning 'spirit' and Barak is a reference to William Barak, the great Wurundjeri leader, whom we honour every time we talk about our work and say the name of the institute.

Our core business at Murrup Barak is around outreach and engagement with future students through schools, community groups and other partners. We also support Aboriginal and Torres Strait Islander students once they enrol with both cultural wraparound support and academic support through tutoring and other academic programs. We are building a sense of community on campus and are also involved in the strategic direction of our business through the Chancellery – including in cultural engagement and operational plans. I also see my role as ensuring that the places where we come to learn are free of racism and are spaces of respect.

It's been tough for students coming out of lockdown because now we have undergraduate students who have had no campus experience. Listening to what their needs are enables us to create programs and events and opportunities that they want to engage in. By creating that sense of community, we can also impart our guidance, our experience and our wisdom. We learn from them. Many of our students have deep cultural knowledge given to them by their Elders. Others haven't yet. They're still on their journey to find where their families are from and are awaiting a time when cultural knowledge will be given to them.

Uncle Pat Dodson teaches us kids – his own kids and his nieces and nephews – that for us as Aboriginal people it's important to only talk about what you know. I also have a responsibility to teach my son and my own nephews and nieces, as well as the students at Murrup Barak, that it's important not to share knowledge unless it's been given to you. We can speak our truth through sharing our lived experience, but it's also important to reflect on the knowledge given by your Elders and to know whether you have permission to share it. If not, then you don't say anything. Ensuring that different pieces of knowledge remain protected and are not skewed in some way is important in maintaining integrity.

Respect and reverence for our Elders is instilled in us from a very young age and is part of the strength of our community. Their knowledge and the experiences that they have had have been different to our own. They are generous with their time and their stories and their guidance and we are humbled to learn from them.

One aspect of my own story is to acknowledge that I have a paler skin than others in my family, and that means I am treated differently by society. Being Black and appearing Black are not the same. I can assert my own identity as a Black woman, but people might look at me and say I look white or I look European. That's their problem. The bigger problem is when racist attitudes overtake people's behaviour. People with darker skin experience the world differently. I'm not followed around in shops because of the way I look, for example. It's important that people understand what racism is and what it isn't. Racism is not something from the past – it continues today and needs to be called out.

Australia was founded as a colony under the lie of *terra nullius*, that this was a land without people. When the attempted genocides began, they laid the foundation for attitudes that continue to this day. When we look at the incarceration rates and the way children continue to be removed from their parents, it's abhorrent, it shouldn't be happening. It's a breach of human rights. Sadly, the system is working exactly as it was designed to. When people talk about the system being broken, it's not. It's running perfectly as it was meant to, which was to continue to diminish us, incarcerate us and kill us off. We're still a long way from the systemic change that will ensure that things could turn around.

I'm really interested to see how the Uluru Statement from the Heart will play out, though I'm not looking forward to the racist sentiment that might come around the campaign. I can't say now if the full acceptance of it will change anything. We do have a voice; we've been talking to this colony for over 200 years. It's the listening that needs to happen, listening and action. I am not an expert on the constitution; nor am I an expert in treaties. But a lot of work is being done through the Uluru Statement and it's important that is translated so everyday people have a full understanding of what is proposed. Dad and Uncle Pat have both worked tirelessly in the past and Uncle Pat, as a Labor senator for Western Australia, has a role in implementing the Uluru Statement from the Heart and is very much committed to it.

We all have a responsibility to our communities to listen and to lead with humility and integrity. When I get older, I don't want my son or my grandkids to ask me why I didn't do anything – or why I didn't do more.

'You influence people by being enthusiastic and putting energy into what you're doing.'

Stephanie Alexander

Living a charmed food life

I always found food wonderfully affirming because I had this exceptional home life based around food. Growing up, almost everybody I knew seemed to eat bland, boring food. I was lucky enough to have a completely different experience, which has moulded my life and given me purpose. Everybody who has spent time with me, whether living together, working together or travelling together, has always been influenced by the way I am around food.

The 1950s were a bleak time food-wise for most Anglo-Australians. My experience was just so different to everybody else's I knew. It used to constantly astonish me what people would eat, their lack of discrimination. Our nightly gathering around the table at home was inextricably linked to the interest my mother had in food. She was as enthusiastic about food as I am. She was way, way ahead of her time.

There were seven of us: Grandpa, Mum and Dad, me and my sister Diana, and my two brothers, John and Christopher. We sat around this beautiful mountain ash table that my father had made. It had a circle of smoky glass in the middle that you lit from underneath. Sometimes Mum put little posies of flowers in it. There was always a parade of delicious things on lovely plates from Mum's eclectic collection of china. And there was always a bottle of wine. Dad loved wine. This, too, was unusual in the 1950s. How many families then would have a bottle of red wine on the table? We didn't drink it as kids, but it was always there.

Mum often produced a little something first and tried all sorts of dishes for the main course. Her rabbit curry is legendary in the family. We all still make it. Her rabbit pie is another favourite – there was a plague of rabbits in our suburb of Rosebud, on Melbourne's Mornington Peninsula.

Mum even had a go at keeping bees and making simple cheeses. She was a very shy person, very tentative, but she was determined to make friends with the local Italian greengrocer and brought broccoli and globe artichokes into our family. Absolutely unheard of! Mum also loved writing about food. She wrote a series of articles in *Australian Gourmet*, now *Gourmet Traveller*. Her way of writing was similar to mine in that she brought in personal experiences to emphasise connections.

Grandpa was as rabid as could be and convinced that every evil in the world came from the United States. He believed the sun shone out of Dad's brother, the journalist Wilfred Burchett.[19] Wilfred was a controversial figure in Australia, staunchly left-wing and a believer in people's right to decide their own destiny. Dad loved him dearly but was more moderate in his views. He was a lifelong member of the Labor Party. He and Grandpa used to have yelling matches at the table. We were used to politics being very much a heated topic of discussion.

Mum and Dad both left school in their early teens. They moved to Rosebud when I was ten and became very involved in the local community. They started a play-reading group and Dad, who was a great reader, lobbied the local council to set up a municipal library.

There were few ratepayer-funded libraries in Australia then, and Victoria's Shire of Flinders set up one of the first. Dad worked there and so did I on Sunday evenings. Dad was also on the local council and the school council. He believed in giving back, in having an impact on your own community. He was an amazing man. I still miss him.

I left home at eighteen to go to university but until then I led a really charmed food life. I still believe in the power of family modelling and am very sad when I realise that for many of today's kids, their family modelling isn't great. Some children have wonderful food and live wonderful middle-class lives, but for a lot of kids, their parents work long, long hours and often don't get any real pleasure out of cooking, buying in ready-made food. There's no way those children are going to have the same experiences as I did, such as sitting at the table with my mother peeling apples together for a delicious pudding.

When I left university and sailed to Europe, I found that food is a window into another culture. I was already in love with France before I ever set foot in the country because I'd read so much about it. I'd certainly read food books, but I'd also read biographies, and when I got there it was exactly what I had hoped. Everybody was interested in what they ate. The food shops were glorious to look at. This was 1960; you didn't have beautiful cheese shops in Australia back then. We do now, but that's sixty years later. French cheese shops were an absolute revelation. I'd never seen anything like them. The patisseries were just as beautiful, as were the bakeries. There was a sense that people had pride in the way they presented their food. And then you'd go to the market and see this absolute proliferation of beautiful, beautiful produce. It was amazing.

I'm a bit of a restaurant junkie, though not so much as I used to be, when I was running restaurants. Most of my friends now don't share my enthusiasm. I understand that and am quite happy to go to an ordinary down-to-earth restaurant, but I'm not interested in bad food, even if it is inexpensive. I love going to extraordinary restaurants. I anticipate it like mad, and when I get there, I want to be made to feel that this is a very special night. I want to be treated beautifully. I don't want music blasting in my ears. It's a joy to go to a quiet restaurant and feel that somebody has really cared about the food, cared about what it looks like. I love that attention to detail.

I wrote my first cookbook, *Stephanie's Menus for Food Lovers*, in 1985, but the book that changed my life, that was my biggest turning point, was *The Cook's Companion* (1996). I put into it everything I knew about food. What prompted me to write it was realising that people didn't understand ingredients. I mean ordinary, regular people who didn't know what you can do with a turnip. I thought I could make a difference. I could show people in a nice friendly way, in good easy prose, exactly the potential of a turnip. So, I started writing and announced to my friend Julie Gibbs at Penguin that I wanted to publish a little paperback of basic ingredients, with a few ideas and a couple of recipes that would be good for people at home. 'Lovely idea,' Julie said. So off I went.

Having trained as a librarian, I started at 'A' and had no intention of diverting to any other letter of the alphabet until I had finished this one. I wrote a little bit about three or four ingredients but kept adding more detail. I kept thinking of something else, such as how to store the ingredients. Then I added suggestions for flavours that go well with those ingredients and then had to give people a couple of ideas on how and what to cook with them. When I had finished my 'A' section, I printed it out and showed it to Julie. She looked aghast at the pile of paper and said she had better talk to the director.

He said, 'Tell her to cut it.' She said, 'I can't do that because it's too good.' I will be forever grateful to Julie for fighting for me.

None of us knew how successful *The Cook's Companion* was going to be. Penguin initially printed 5000 copies of this 800-page book, sold at $75 a copy. It was a phenomenal success. Within a week, the whole 5000 had sold, and the book had to be reprinted twice before Christmas. To this day it still sells. It has given me financial security. When it was first published, in 1996, Melbourne was struggling out of the recession we had to have. I had a lot of debts, and my royalties meant that I could leave Stephanie's Restaurant with my head held high and every obligation paid for.

At about the time *The Cook's Companion* came out, I was very aware that there was a national conversation going on about children and food. All sorts of well-meaning people, usually nutritionists or health professionals, wanted to talk about food groups and nutrition. I just knew that was the wrong way to influence children's food habits, that there was a better way of doing it – which was to develop a well-rounded program that every kid, no matter their interests, their background, shape or age, would enjoy. I understood what was really needed was a program that took place in schools, that was super enjoyable and that emphasised the pleasure associated with food as well as the holistic angle – the understanding about planting and growth, sustainability and so on. All this without making it dry and boring and concentrating on food groups and designating what is good for you, what is bad. So that's what I did.

You influence people by being enthusiastic and putting energy into what you're doing. When I was running my own restaurants, I did this with my apprentices. They loved it. My enthusiasm around food has never been lacking. I have always been able to bring together a group of people to support me with new ideas, which I did with my restaurants and which I did when setting up the Kitchen Garden Foundation. People were influenced by my enthusiasm and energy but didn't necessarily have a lot of money, so setting up the foundation was and still is an exercise in keeping funded.

The program started in 2001 at Collingwood College in Melbourne. There are now more than a thousand schools involved. That includes a growing number of early learning centres. We have different programs for the early learners, for primary schools and for secondary schools. We do have some secondary schools that say they want to be part of our scheme and more enlightened secondary-school teachers who can see how they can mould the official curriculum to include this.

The social behaviour of the children involved in the program is amazing. They work in small teams; they liaise with one another and all get on wonderfully well. In the program, kids are learning not only how to handle a knife or how to plant a seed in the garden, but how to be with other people and how to actually love it. I have just been to northern New South Wales and Tasmania to visit schools using the program. It was fantastic to see the kids making decisions and doing things like cooking their own pasta. What they're getting in the Kitchen Garden program is an understanding about food diversity, learning a new vocabulary, learning how to measure, how to weigh, how to estimate, and above all how to taste and to bring joy to their daily life. They set the table most beautifully: they put flowers on the table and then they sat around the table. One of the biggest shocks I had with the Kitchen Garden Foundation was finding that for so many children, sitting round a table is a new experience. They just don't do it and their parents are modelling poor eating habits. The family often eat sitting on the couch with the television on. Then there are those children who eat at different times to their parents because parents get home so late, thus missing out on the great or revealing conversations that happen at the family table.

Whenever I go to a school, I get overwhelmed with the stories. The volunteers, the teacher, the principal, the parents (if they are involved) all say versions of the same thing: that the children have a totally different attitude to food now. They're much more prepared to try something they haven't seen before and they understand they won't like everything the first time. So I know the program is valuable. One little kid ran after me at Cobargo Primary School as I was leaving with Kristy McBain, federal Minister for Regional Development, Local Government and Territories. This little boy said, 'Thank you so much for starting the program. It's my favourite bit of school.'

'You might grow up to be a chef or a gardener,' I told him.

'Well, I think so!' he replied.

Kristy McBain was knocked out.

The foundation has a staff of twenty and a board. We have a new CEO, Dr Cathy Wilkinson. The biggest challenge is finding the funding. We have established a corporate partnership with Coles supporting every school doing the program in Tasmania. Coles offer customers the chance to donate $2 to the schools every time they shop.

The Kitchen Garden Foundation wouldn't have been possible without the success of *The Cook's Companion*. It gave me an income so I didn't have to get another job. It meant I could devote 100 per cent of my time and energy to establishing the foundation: lobbying on its behalf; travelling to meet politicians, to meet this person and that person; trying to keep it afloat; applying for grants. What was lovely for me was that even to this day, wherever I go I get compliments from people. I've even been given books to sign with no backs on them. They apologise for this, but I tell them I love it when I can see the book's been well used.

It would be fair to say I haven't had huge success in my emotional life. My first husband, Monty, and I were very happy together, but we exhausted ourselves with hard work running our first restaurant, Jamaica House, and our marriage didn't last long. Our daughter, Lisa, had a tough time. My second marriage, to barrister Maurice Alexander, didn't work out either, but did produce another daughter, Holly. I love my girls very much and nowadays we spend time together as a priority, sharing stories and holidays.

I am deeply grateful for the upbringing I had because it set a standard. It gave me a love of reading and an understanding that there was no such thing as only one way of doing things, that there is always another way, and that food is one of the great joys in life and is accessible to most people. It doesn't have to be expensive. I remember overhearing two women once at a writers' festival where I had been giving a talk about a book I had written. 'Food writers!' one of them said. 'They'll have gardeners next.'

I thought, *How much you are missing out on …*

'I would like to see the importance of appropriate accommodation for people with mental illness recognised more substantially on a national level.'

Allan Fels

Advocating for housing for those with mental illness

I almost had a brilliant career in politics. When I was studying economics and law at the University of Western Australia in the early 1960s, I was quite friendly with another, older, law student. One morning, as we were walking out of a lecture, he told me he was president of the local branch of the Liberal Party in the exclusive suburb of Nedlands and was going to have to resign at a meeting the next day because of some problem and would I like to take over from him? I told him I would think about it, that I didn't mind that it was Liberal. My family was Liberal. He said it would cost me five pounds to become a member – a lot in those days. I agreed and signed up.

The next day at 5.00 pm we turned up at the Nedlands branch. My friend announced that he was resigning and nominated me to replace him. Someone seconded the motion and that was it – all over in five minutes. I was the newly elected president of the Nedlands branch of the Liberal Party at the age of twenty-one.

I spent the next two years heavily involved in the West Australian division of the Liberal Party as well as in student politics at university, where I was president of the Guild of Undergraduates, following in the footsteps of H.C. 'Nugget' Coombs and Bob Hawke. My older brother had dabbled a bit in student politics, and I learnt a great deal from him.

With the Liberals, I was elected secretary of the Curtin division, a federal seat represented by Paul Hasluck in Canberra. Nedlands was then represented in the West Australian parliament by Charles Court, who was to become premier in 1974. I could easily have got into parliament if I'd waited, but then, after getting my degree, I was offered a scholarship to Duke University in North Carolina. This turned me in a different direction to politics, though my education in political and procedural skills has been helpful throughout my career.

Law and economics were an unusual combination to study at university. The two disciplines are very, very different. Law tends to focus on the individual and their rights, whereas economics is utilitarian: it looks at the economic system and how things work in that framework and is not too concerned with individual rights. It's more concerned with making sure that everyone is playing their part in the system, irrespective of their rights.

After Duke, I went to Cambridge as a research fellow. I found the work dull but eventually was offered a fantastic job that changed my life. It involved working with Professor H.A. 'Bert' Turner in producing an independent study of the UK National Board for Prices and Incomes. My report became a book, *The British Prices and Incomes Board* (1972), and was a huge success. It set me on the course of my professional life.

Another turning point came after Cambridge, when I was back to Australia and working at Monash University. The late Maureen Brunt, Professor of Economics, suggested that we do some teaching together, running a new course in competition and regulation. She did competition, I did regulation. I had seen them as separate fields but thanks to her we integrated and suddenly I got into the world of competition and became a true believer. That set my path for many years and gave me a framework for thinking about it.

Once I went into practice as a regulator in the field of competition, partly by accident, I just didn't have time to follow the academic side. Fifty years ago, you got people who could happily combine both, but these days you're so busy in a regulatory job you can't keep up with the best academic work, and vice versa.

When I became a price regulator at the Australian Competition and Consumer Commission (ACCC), I exposed myself to all the people who thought regulating prices was not a smart approach. Instead, they had another idea altogether about competition. I discovered that getting a lot of criticism from powerful institutions like banks or oil companies is actually a plus in the minds of the public. People come up to you in the street and hail you as a hero, irrespective of the merits of what you did. I didn't mind being labelled as one of the most powerful men in Australia at that time. I certainly saw the value of using the media. I also saw the risks and it was okay. I got away with it; not all people do. I think I read the power situation correctly, that the ACCC's a place where you can go out on a limb without really sacrificing your position.

My most significant turning point personally was my daughter Isabella's diagnosis of schizophrenia. She'd had a very difficult childhood and early adulthood and her behaviour was often bizarre, eccentric and embarrassing. She wasn't happy at school but had many escape mechanisms, living her own internal, slightly unusual, mental life and different perceptions of things. But in the mid-1990s, when she was twenty-five, things changed. She experienced severe psychosis: voices in her head shouting unpleasant things, gunshots going off in her mind and a severe inability to understand anything going on in the world around her. It was a huge shock, but it meant we could make sense of the situation and start proper medication and treatment.

We were very aware at the time of the widespread belief that mental illness was caused by the family. I think this unduly influenced the many psychotherapy psychiatrists and even psychologists we saw. A more sophisticated version was the view that psychoanalysis will solve it when there's obviously a strong chemical imbalance factor to be addressed, among other things. Even to this day it's very unclear what is the best approach for the treatment of people with mental illness. Some people emphasise the medical, some social housing, some cognitive therapy.

Initially I was very concerned not to make Isabella's diagnosis public as I was a public figure. I feared it would be used against me as there was a big media campaign being conducted at the time by the Murdoch press – we rejected some of their mergers. They threw everything at me, so I kept it quiet, and for a year or two we thought Isabella would be cured. But it became more and more apparent that this was going to be a lifelong problem for her.

My late wife, Maria-Isabel, made the care of Isabella her focus. It was very difficult living with her at home, but when she was living elsewhere that didn't work well either. Isabel gave a great deal of thought as to the ideal living arrangements for people with severe persistent schizophrenia. She had relatives who had schizophrenia so had deeper insight. She was very supportive of all of us as a family.

I was under a lot of pressure dealing with the ACCC job, a lot of it pretty unpleasant. But I've always been a very calm, stable person. I get through most things without getting too upset. I was away from home a great deal but always took Isabella's phone calls, no matter who I kept waiting.

In 2002, we discussed going public as a family. Isabella was in full agreement and we chose *Australian Story*. I realised I could use my profile to raise public awareness and understanding of mental illness. After our story went to air, some parents who also had children with severe mental illnesses contacted us and together we formulated the idea of setting up a model where people with mental illness would live independently in self-contained apartments yet be part of a community and have access to onsite staff. We called it the Haven. We set up an entity called the Haven Foundation in 2006 and pressed governments and a few foundations for financial support.

We were fortunate that the Catholic parish in South Yarra, Melbourne, had a disused convent that they were about to sell for a very large sum of money but decided instead to put it to good social use and give it to us at a very low cost. Then, after heavy lobbying over three years, we got money from the Victorian government to renovate the rundown building and turn it into fourteen apartments with the old convent courtyard and garden forming communal areas. It was an ideal solution and opened in 2011. To this day it operates successfully.

When I see the improvements in Isabella and other Haven residents, I'm convinced we need to adopt this model much more widely. Stable, secure, long-term accommodation greatly improves everyone's mental health, especially those with mental illness. When mentally ill people go into hospital, they are given medication, but they need more than that. They need somewhere to live that's stable and secure, otherwise they are susceptible to relapse, exploitation, self-harm and suicide. Accommodation alone is not the answer; nor is medication alone. They need both.

Through the Haven Foundation we pressed governments, philanthropists and charitable foundations for support in getting

TURNING POINTS

more Havens. We now have Haven residences operating in Victoria in Frankston, Epping, Geelong, Laverton and Mooroopna. More are being built at Pakenham, Drouin, Seymour, Ballarat and North Bendigo. Eventually we hope to have twenty or thirty. That's a lot of lives turned around.

I would like to see the importance of appropriate accommodation for people with mental illness recognised more substantially on a national level and to raise public awareness of mental illness generally. Attitudes are still poor, particularly towards people at the severe end. With less serious illnesses such as depression, anxiety and personality disorders, there has been an improvement in public attitudes, which is good. But not with schizophrenia – not yet. We've still got a long way to go.

'Sculptures will be there for hundreds of years, speaking to those who stop and look ... It's not about whether people remember me or not, but about the works themselves putting good messages out into the world.'

Meliesa Judge

Finding inspiration in bronze

As a sculptor I have a strong sense of purpose, but art wasn't my life ambition growing up. I was planning to be a doctor. I'm not sure how much that idea was mine or my parents'. It was something I had always had in my mind, that I took for granted.

We lived in Adelaide in a household of books and musical instruments, no television, intellectually alive. My father was an academic; the books were his. Poetry, art, literature all lined the walls on handmade wooden shelves with three layers of varnish, smooth as velvet. I remember him making these in his shed while I, a four-year-old, clamped offcut chunks of timber into the vice and carved shapes with his old wood files. Rough metal and wood in my hands was an early memory.

My mother worked at Flinders Medical Centre as personal assistant to Professor Anthony Radford, who was also a long-time family friend. Just as I was about to enrol in medicine at university, I had a conversation with him that changed my life. It was my turning point. He said, 'If you have a talent in the arts, it's worth exploring. That there are a lot of people who are capable of being good doctors but not many people who are capable of being good artists.'

I have no idea why he said that, but he'd known me since I was a child and perhaps felt he knew me well enough. It made me pause: I decided to take a 'gap year' and go to art school rather than straight into medicine. I went to the School of Art and Design at Underdale in South Australia – not the most exciting experience. Art school was a bit of a human zoo in the mid-1980s: it was all blue mohawks, pub culture, a lot of drug problems. But I fell in love with ceramics, sculpture and hot glass, and with my future husband, Will Kuiper, who was nearing the end of a four-year art course. I never got too far with the hot glass as I was too shy to accept the surprise offer of a glass-blowing traineeship at JamFactory in Adelaide. And medicine? It just drifted out of my focus, it literally drifted. I kept thinking I would enrol the next year, but that next year never came as I got more and more involved in art.

I left art school in 1987 and took a job with Artlab, a major conservation centre closely linked with the South Australian Museum and Art Gallery of South Australia. It gave me practical and inspirational art training and a rich experience helping to restore objects that were thousands of years old, including Aboriginal artefacts and Egyptian bronzes.

After leaving art school, I shared a group studio with other artists. The creation of art gradually grew in importance for me. When my Artlab contract came up for renewal, I was ready to dive deeply into a disciplined studio practice and to brave a world that would either accept or reject me according to the bare and honest essentials of a competitive marketplace.

Will and I made a very clear decision that we would be doing sculpture full-time. It was a huge financial risk, while at the same time a leap of faith. I don't think I would be doing it if I wasn't in partnership with Will. Working in bronze is so complex, such hard work, and uses up copious doses of ingenuity. You need strong moral support and that's what we give each other.

Will has always put my projects front and centre. He's always taken me very seriously, which is important to me. That is how our company, Liquid Metal Studios, has grown into something quite substantial. We lease a disused council depot in the foothills of the Mount Lofty Ranges, in which we combine a small office, a studio, a workshop, foundry and gallery.

There are women in Australia who are sculpting, but I don't know any women who are running a foundry and casting their own work. There are women working in foundries, but very few and they're not in charge, whereas Will and I run Liquid Metals Studio together. We're an equal couple.

The journey of a sculpture begins with a commission. One of my first major commissions was a life-size sculpture of Mary Ward, founder of the Loreto Institute. She was a seventeenth-century Yorkshire woman who understood the importance of education for women. The Loretos have seven schools in Australia and wanted a cast of the Mary Ward sculpture installed in every one.

The Loretos approached a few artists and asked us to submit a maquette – a small-scale model. They saw something in mine that convinced them that I was working towards what they were looking for. When they gave me the commission, I spent months researching Mary Ward, reading her writings and talking to the Loreto sisters before signing the contract. My final maquette showed Mary Ward striding out, a pack on her back, the embodiment of the Loreto spirit. She's very much my girl!

TURNING POINTS

I love to do work that is meaningful, that resounds profoundly with many people. The challenge with the Mary Ward sculpture was that each girl in the school, from primary to Year 12, will see it two or three times a day every day of their school life. That's thousands and thousands of times. The first time you see a sculpture you consciously react, you respond, but gradually the effect wears off. Gradually, it will turn into a piece of furniture. You don't consciously think about it anymore, but your eyes are still registering that image and it's having an impact. I know this because it happens to me. I will be working on a sculpture, go and have lunch, and when I come back I get the feeling there's someone there and I jump. It's the sculpture. So subliminally, even when you're not actively thinking about it, in the back recesses of your brain, you are still getting that message – whatever that message is that we've written into the form and shape and moment and movement of that sculpture.

So finding the valid message is the key. What the Mary Ward sculpture is saying to those schoolgirls is that it is okay to step out, to be strong, independent, powerfully spiritual and active, whereas our society tends to put out the message that women need to be really pretty and really skinny.

The Mary Ward sculpture brought me a number of commissions with a religious theme, including life-sized sculptures of Catherine McAuley, the nineteenth-century Irish founder of the Sisters of Mercy and great humanitarian, and Ignatius of Loyola, the sixteenth-century founder of the Jesuits, a Spanish nobleman and soldier who laid down his sword and exchanged clothes with a beggar. I believe sculptures are like poems. They take the big themes and distil them down to concentrates. I want the work to dive deep into a place of universal wisdom, to the shared well of knowledge. Each of these figures has a sense of the singular human search: Mary Ward seeking active spirituality and education for women and girls; Catherine McAuley addressing the need for compassion and shelter; Ignatius, a powerful and angry man, laying down his weapons and symbolically renouncing violence.

A very different sculpture to these heroic religious figures was that of a water bird with outstretched wings watching over a nesting mother and several baby birds. It was commissioned by Christine Heard, whose husband had died very suddenly of leukaemia. She was raw with grief and came with a very clear idea of what she wanted. She had chosen a peaceful place beside a pond in the Waite Arboretum at the University of Adelaide Waite Campus in Urrbrae.

The following year I was working on another sculpture in that same park, some distance from the waterbirds, when I noticed a frail old man in a wheelchair being pushed by his carer down the path to the pond, where he sat for half an hour just looking at the bronze birds. While I was watching him, I realised that sculpture has a whole lot of different meanings and references, that everything you do is going to have a completely different resonance for other people and it's not necessarily what I've put into it that carries this. Seeing that brought home to me how important the work is.

As an artist I struggled to put the meaning of it into words until I came across a quote from Alain de Botton about religious art in his book *Religion for Atheists* (2012). He wrote that the purpose of making art for some people, people like me, is that the eyes educate the mind, the eyes educate the heart. So, for some people, when they see something beautiful or evocative or passionate, that brings the message home when all the words in the world will not reach them.[20]

TURNING POINTS

I draw my own spiritual strength from living on a beautiful ten-acre block in the Adelaide Hills. It's an ancient piece of land with old rocks and remnant bush, a very spiritual corner of the world. I can spend twelve hours there and come back to the studio with enough energy for a week. We are sustained brilliantly by living on very little. Accepting the reality of a low income buys us time to be alive and do stuff, rather than buy stuff. Our furniture and clothes are second-hand but our lives and souls are not.

For fun and social contact, Will and I go swing dancing every week in central Adelaide. It makes a great break from the solitary intensity and physical demands of our work. I recently had a conversation with a young woman there, a medical intern, whom I hadn't spoken to before. When I said I was a sculptor, she told me the first sculpture she knew anything about was at her school. She remembered the woman who created it coming to her class and telling the students how it was made. She said she saw that sculpture every day and found it inspiring.

It turned out the school was Loreto College Marryatville and the sculpture was my Mary Ward. It was just one of those moments reminding me that those sculptures will be there for hundreds of years, speaking to those who stop and look. I hope they just keep communicating. It's not about whether people remember me or not, but about the works themselves putting good messages out into the world.

It's incredible to have a companion to walk the path with you. The work is so gruelling – there are such big disappointments and such large hurdles to overcome – that if you're not working with someone who's completely in sympathy with you it would be heartbreaking. There have been many moments when Will and I have almost walked away from sculpting and each time something has pulled us back. We walk a fine line between joy and disaster.

At one time we were at the beginning of a bronze casting and things kept going wrong. Something we were due to deliver went terribly wrong and instead of starting again, we just took two weeks off. I remember walking around Uluru and making the serious decision that if the next cast didn't work, I would never cast again. *That's it, it's too hard,* I thought. So we went back and cast it again and it was perfect. There wasn't the smallest flaw in it. And we thought, *Damn, now we have to keep going!*

'I think that kindness is one of the most underrated and underestimated qualities.'

Jane Rowe

Ensuring that every child has a childhood

In the late 1990s I was working at Windana, the drug and alcohol rehabilitation centre in St Kilda, when something happened that totally changed my life.

I had been there a few years and at that stage was an assessment officer – which meant that people would come in and I would assess their suitability for treatment before putting them on the waiting list for admission. The waiting lists were huge, and invariably when people called in, usually once a week I would have to say, 'Sorry, there's still no bed for you.' People would overdose and die waiting.

This particular day, four friends I was seeing regularly came in. They had been on the waiting list for weeks and I had to tell them there were still no beds. They said they were going to go out and get stoned that night. I said, 'I can't stop you, but if you're going to do that, you've got to stick together because there's some very strong heroin out there at the moment. People are overdosing and if you're by yourself, you'll quite likely die.'

So the four of them went out that night, used heroin and passed out. Two of them woke up, two didn't. The two who didn't were both young mums. I knew their kids. I remember going into Windana the next day and being told what had happened. I was devastated. I felt completely redundant in my role because unless you can get people immediate help, they're in danger of dying.

I went to the funeral of one of the young mums. It was a Thursday. It's etched in my memory. Her parents were there – they hadn't seen their daughter for years. Her son, who was about six, was sitting in the front row with a social worker. Her parents had no idea he existed. He loved his mum and she had loved him; she was his world. At the end of the service, as they lowered the coffin, he went running up, crying uncontrollably and yelling, 'Where are you putting my mummy? Where are you putting my mummy?' It was heartbreaking.

The little boy was led away by a social worker he didn't know. I'm sure she was a good person but regardless, he had no one and would have been placed in emergency care. I just thought, *This kid is going to be so much more likely to use drugs himself later to block out his grief and trauma or may attempt suicide. Why are we waiting till someone's in trouble?* I lay awake all night with those thoughts in my head, asking myself what I could do. That's when it came to me that we need to have an organisation supporting kids. There was no one doing it. Whether a child ended up in foster care or some other form of residential care, there was no specific support for them.

The next day I rang a musician friend, Spencer P. Jones, about putting on a benefit concert to raise enough money to buy Christmas presents for the kids I knew through Windana whose mum or dad had died or had abandoned them through drug use. We spent the weekend on the phone and by Monday had a two-night concert organised because every musician we spoke to immediately agreed to be part of it.

Very early on, things started snowballing. In the process of organising the concert I began to realise how great the needs were. I discovered, for example, that if the children were being cared for by a blood relative, that relative was not entitled to any government support. So our mission grew organically. We wanted our message to be absolutely clear: this concert was to raise money for children orphaned or abandoned due to parental drug use and who were in the care of extended family, generally grandparents.

Mirabel was founded within a week of that funeral. I had huge support, especially from Peter Bucci, the inspirational founder of Windana, to whom I was very close. He understood why I wanted to set up a new charity for the children and that it had to be separate from Windana. He also offered that until we were legally organised, we could operate under the auspices of Windana to qualify for tax deductibility. He gave me twenty-four hours to come up with a name, and I thought of Mirabel immediately. I remembered a story I was told by the nuns at my convent primary school in England about a saintly woman called Mirabel who lived in France and looked after abandoned and unwanted children. She never turned a child away. It synchronised perfectly with my vision that every child deserves a childhood. We had the name by Monday.

Peter's experience in setting up Windana was invaluable. We had to find out what setting up a not-for-profit charity involved, such as getting tax deductibility status, coping with complex legal issues and writing a constitution. We had three months to organise ourselves before the concert. There were twelve of us from different worlds – music, the law, youth work – all determined to make it happen. We met at my home on Thursday nights. The deal was I supplied the food and they rocked up. There was a lot of passion and positive energy and fun. It wasn't heavy. So right from the start I was surrounded by good people. They each had a vital role to play. Donald Mack, my ex-brother-in-law, ran the funds management section of a large insurance company. He was happy to advise me even though at that stage we had no funds. Others included Simon Northeast, a criminal lawyer who did a lot of work with drug addicts; Jay Jordens, a youth worker with a group called Connections; and Rebecca Barnard, a singer. It was that group of twelve people who thrashed it all out, worked out a plan and got it up and running.

It's a bit like a plane going down: you're told to put the oxygen mask on yourself before putting it on your child. We had to help these family members and give them the energy and support they needed, so one of the first things we did was set up support groups for grandparents, aunts and uncles. We not only met face to face but also were there at the end of the phone to talk to them, hear them, share our knowledge. Our research showed us that this was where we could make the biggest difference.

The concert took place in December 1998 and was a brilliant success. It morphed into an annual event known as 'Music, Mirth & Mayhem' at the Melbourne International Comedy Festival, which continued until recently. Some of the musicians who took part in that first concert, like Deborah Conway, have been involved with Mirabel ever since. With the money we raised, we did buy the kids great Christmas presents, and there was enough left over for a fax machine for the office.

The foundation just sort of grew organically, there was such a need for a service like this. It filled a huge gap. Our first office was a room in my home. I was trying to juggle my job at Windana with getting Mirabel up and running. Word got out very quickly. I had been working in the field for years and had a lot of contacts. We attracted some funding from the Felton Bequest, thanks to Bruce Bonyhady and Sir Gustav Nossal, who heard about what we were doing. Triple J picked us up for their annual Real Appeal. The government heard about us through that. We got a call from a federal government department and I had a meeting with an amazing man called Peter Quick and his offsider. We sat around my kitchen table and talked. They offered some funding, confident that I wouldn't be working from home forever. As a result of the funding, we could advertise for a project manager and Nicole Patton joined Mirabel. She became my right hand and still works with Mirabel.

Nicole and I used to do home visits and very soon we were running support groups for grandparents, renting a room in Chapel Off Chapel in Prahan. They were grappling with issues such as: *should I take my grandchild to their mum's funeral? Should I take my grandchild to visit their dad in prison? Why is my grandchild wetting the bed at the age of eight?* One of the first things we did when we opened our official office eighteen months later, over a plumbing shop in Ripponlea, was to create a resource book for kinship carers in which we deal with these and other questions facing families. It's packed with invaluable information such as the law relating to the care of children and helpful contacts such as the Child Care Access Hotline. We've just updated and reissued that book twenty years later![21]

We've always been careful not to start something without being confident we can see it through. I'm so aware that, working with kids with abandonment issues, we don't want to start anything and then a year later go, *Sorry, we can't afford to do that anymore.* Similarly, we've never gone to people with our hand out if we don't really fit the bill. I think we've stayed very true to who we are and what we do even though issues change all the time and our culture changes all the time.

In the early stages of setting up Mirabel, I picked up the paper one morning and saw an article about John Fogarty, a Family Court judge who was retiring. I rang his chambers and by sheer chance he happened to be there. I asked him if he would be our patron. He invited me to come to his house that afternoon to talk about it, which I did, and I was thrilled when he agreed. It was a big thing for him to do and he was fantastic.

When I left Windana, I was seeing probably fourth-generation drug use and unemployment. The drug culture now is vastly different and much more prolific. There's more despair and serious issues of homelessness and poverty, of not having a role model, of not having an education. Addiction is generally about some form of avoidance or trauma, but I think there's probably a lot more for people to want to avoid now and much less hope for young people. Mirabel is all about hope and belonging. You might be heartbroken by a child's background and circumstances, but you go, *Hey, I can improve this.*

We get at least one child referred to us every day – that's seven every week. We're currently caring for around 2000 children. Over the years we've cared for thousands of children, many of whom we keep in touch with. Once a kid turns eighteen, we officially close their file. Some are now working with us as volunteers, running groups that they were once part of as young children. They still call themselves Mirabel kids and when they turn eighteen they join our alumni program. They're incredibly proud to be part of this extended Mirabel family.

It is moving beyond measure to see how Mirabel kids grow. We've got some amazing young people among our alumni. One of them is Ashlee, a beautiful young woman who has been involved with us since she was eight. She had a horrific childhood and was badly treated by many of her mum's boyfriends. She eventually ran away from home. Her mum died a couple of years ago from a drug overdose. Ashlee got up to speak at the funeral and said, 'She wasn't the best mum, but she was my mum.' This is a young person who's been through a lot, but part of what Mirabel tries to do is help our kids make sense of their childhood and to say to them, *You weren't to blame.*

Another child who was faced with horrific, horrific stuff was Heaven. She adored her nan, who died quite young. Heaven felt it was because of the grief her mum caused and she was filled with anger. I worked with Heaven for years and years. She hit depression as a teenager and we supported her through that. When she left school, she got a job with a travel agent in London and we had dinner together one evening when I was visiting the United Kingdom. She said, 'Janie, I've been thinking a lot about things, about what we talked about, about my own journey and my depression and I suddenly thought, *Maybe Mum suffered depression too and no one understood it. Maybe that's why she turned to drugs.* And you know what, Janie? I'm not angry with her anymore.'

It's just as well that when we started all those years ago I had no idea how Mirabel would grow because I would have been overwhelmed. We've become a huge extended family and from the start attracted incredible support. It's been organic. Someone would offer us some funding which meant that, for example, we could bring on another member of staff. We could see the need for camps for the kids, and money was given to us to rent a respite place in the country. In 2019, thanks to generous supporters, we moved into our own magnificently restored and furnished building in St Kilda. We have thirty-two on the staff here now and dozens of volunteers. We also have an office in Newcastle, New South Wales.

At the beginning I just wanted to make a difference in some capacity. I think that kindness is one of the most underrated and underestimated qualities. When I went to the funeral of that young mother in 1998, I thought if I could just give a Christmas present to kids like that little boy, they would know they were special. It was just simple kindness.

'To succeed I had to be different while staying true to who I was.'

Peter Sharp

Seeing life through a lens

The biggest and most profound turning point in my life was in mid-2011. It was also my breaking point. I was standing in the middle of Macquarie Shopping Centre in Sydney on the phone to a claims assessor, chasing him up regarding my disability claim with his insurance company. It wasn't a pleasant conversation. I was frustrated. The company had been applying the strategy of delay, delay, delay, stuff me around, try to get rid of me. I think it was partly a strategy to see if I could return to work. If I could have, I would have done so, but I was unemployable. I couldn't function.

The claims assessor started getting annoyed with me and said, 'Peter, we're never going to pay you, so if you can't go back to work, what is the point in you living?'

Something in me broke. I burst into tears. I remember thinking, *You're right. What is my purpose? What is my point? If I can't return to work, what am I meant to do?*

This conversation took place after a lifetime of pain that had got dramatically worse over the previous year. As a child in Western Australia, I was involved in four car accidents and as a result had always had issues with pain in my back, my spine, my body. However, it was only in early 2010 that the pain got to the point where it became unbearable. I was thirty-one. MRIs from April through to June showed that I had multiple damaged discs in my back, and they were getting worse. Then in June one of those discs herniated and left me in incredible pain, though I didn't realise what was causing it. I thought it was muscle pain.

This happened while I was overseas for a week's work in Korea and Japan. I managed to see the week out, but when I got on the plane to come home, I was weeping with pain. I'd lost a lot of the feeling in my left leg. I remember lying on the floor in the Qantas lounge in Tokyo talking to my boss and drinking sake, as much sake as I could get, to numb the pain. Once I was back in Sydney, I saw a neurosurgeon and was operated on within four days. Unfortunately, I picked the wrong surgeon, who picked the wrong operation. I was only meant to be in hospital for a couple of days but was there for three and a bit weeks.

I worked in the electronics industry and went back after three months because they told me I wouldn't have a job otherwise. So I returned, full of painkillers. I was taking Valium, Endone, Lyrica, gabapentin and ENDEP. I was also on OxyContin for a long time, and then a fentanyl patch, as well as antidepressants. These drugs messed with my body, messed with my system, messed with my head.

The scary thing is that you get to a point with pain medication where you can appear to function quite well, but those few months when I was back to work, I was pretty stoned. Eventually my company did the right thing by me and made me redundant. So I was jobless and burning through my savings. I remember going to Centrelink and scoring twenty out of twenty in the test they give to judge how disabled you are. I was given a disability sticker but copped a lot of abuse because I don't look disabled. People's perception around disability often involves a wheelchair, but it extends beyond physical disability. For me, it's the mental side of chronic pain that I struggle with every day.

My wife, Nicola, and I spent the next year going from one doctor, one specialist, one therapist, to another. It was very much the two of us doing it together. I spent a lot of time in bed staring at the ceiling, but I didn't just sit back and feel sorry for myself. I did hydrotherapy and physio, I did quite a bit of exercise. One specialist we saw wanted to fuse my spine in a couple of places, but I knew that would involve more surgery down the track. It wasn't something I wanted to sign up for. Then one of the specialists discovered there was something we were unaware of happening in my body, something much more sinister than damaged discs. It was arthritic in nature.

All the while I was fighting my claim with the insurance company in relation to my disability cover. They were being really evil. It's the only word I can use to describe them: evil. That phone call in Macquarie Shopping Centre was my lowest point. I couldn't see a way through. The pain became mental, then I became suicidal. That scared me. When I can see a path to the future, when I can see what that looks like, mentally I'm okay. When I can't see a path, when I can't see a way forward, I can't cope. My brain is very black and white; it doesn't work in grey.

I broke but was determined to mend, which meant working out how to live with pain and how to live without painkillers. Coming off medication takes a huge toll. Battling through that every day takes away your joy. It's not something you should do unsupervised, so I checked into a couple of places. One was really bad and I came out worse than when I went in. The other was really good. I learned mindfulness, I learned detachment, I learned to picture the pain as a passenger on a bus, and I was the bus. The pain wasn't who I am.

TURNING POINTS

It was around this time that I picked up my camera again – my grandfather had given me my first camera when I was thirty – and started taking photos. It was kind of art therapy. I've always been creative, and photography has always been a hobby, but at some point the idea that this could provide me with an income kicked in. It became my passion, especially taking photos of animals. We lived in beautiful hill country forty minutes east of Perth and have always had animals. At different times they have included rabbits, cats, birds, a dog, fish, mice and a rat. I was born with an affinity with animals and dreamed of becoming a vet. I didn't have the marks when I left school and so switched to another love, music, and became an audio engineer in the music industry instead.

I tried every type of photography, and it was a natural step to go back to the music industry and shoot musicians. I loved capturing the explosive, primal feeling of a live show as well as the charisma of performers such as Lorde, Bon Iver, Foo Fighters, Soundgarden, Florence and the Machine. But the lifestyle wasn't good for my back, especially the late hours, the crush. I was working with paparazzi-type photographers, some of whom I liked, some who were not pleasant to be around.

Driving back from the Byron Bay Bluesfest in 2015, I started thinking to myself, *Why are you doing this? You're not enjoying it, it's taking a toll on your body and there's little financial benefit.* I decided to make a change. I thought of my love for animals and wondered how I could specialise in animal photography. I looked at what other pet photographers were doing and I realised that because of my disability, I had to be different. I'm very limited in terms of how much work I can do and how long I can function. To succeed I had to be different while staying true to who I was.

160

In time (it took four years) the insurance company paid, and I bought a house in the Sydney suburb of Belrose. Friends helped me convert my double garage into a studio with an adjacent office, and Tame & Wild Studio opened officially in February 2017. For the first few months I didn't have many clients. I didn't have my processes sorted, I didn't have my marketing sorted. I did a few weddings, portraits and music gigs as well as pets, but from early 2018 I focused exclusively on animals.

My point of difference is the way I relate to animals. I gain their trust and help them relax when their owners bring them to the studio. I talk to the owners about what their pet means to them, which helps me to frame the animal's personality. I'm really patient. I take my time, which can be anywhere from twenty minutes to an hour before I start taking photos. There's always going to be stress when you put an animal into a new environment. Having fun and playing games makes a difference, as does having a capacity to read them, to connect with them. My favourite animals to photograph are chickens. They have the most amazing personalities. They just perform. They dance, they show off, they have attitude.

Once I had the business established, I decided I wanted to be an ambassador for the welfare of animals by volunteering for a day a week with one pet shelter and one wildlife rescue. To my surprise, it took a while to find a pet rescue home that wanted me. A lot of the rescuers I spoke to were either rude or uninterested, and I understand why. When you see what humans do to animals, you develop a need to protect them.

It was actually a little disheartening, but I persevered and found the Sydney Dogs and Cats Home. I applied as a volunteer and was accepted. On my first day I met Melody. She had been almost literally starved to death, she was skin and bones. She was petrified – still alive, but barely. I cried while taking photos of Melody and reached a point where I had to stop. I just said, *This is enough. This dog is distressed. I am distressed.* I photographed a lot of animals that day, but it was Melody who stayed in my head. I told Nicola that seeing what humans can do to animals was beyond awful. I found it hard to go back.

Three weeks later, I photographed Melody again. She had been with temporary foster carers and was a totally different dog. She looked amazing – she had put on weight and she had lots of energy. Seeing her transformation in such a short time gave me the idea for a book of before and after photos and stories of rescue dogs. I signed a publishing deal with Macmillan at the end of 2018 and, together with the staff at the home, started collecting material.

Lost But Found came out in time for Christmas 2019, with royalties going to the Sydney Dogs and Cats Home. The book tells the stories of forty dogs, many of which came to the home hungry, homeless, sick, frightened, flea-ridden and broken. The before photos show these vulnerable animals as they are when they arrive at the shelter, and the before stories explain how they came to be there. The after photos show the healing of the animals' bodies and spirits due to the love and care lavished on them in the home. The after stories tell how new owners were found, often in response to my photos, and the impact the dogs have on the people who rescue them – like bull-Arab-staffy-cross Sasha, who was adopted by Taylor. 'I saved her,' she said, 'but really she saved me.'

There is often an instant connection between dogs and prospective adopters. Adam and Natalie Goodes, for example, wanted to give an older dog a home and met lots of loud boisterous candidates at the Sydney Dogs and Cats Home, but it wasn't till they saw a shy, sad-looking staffy cross curled up in a corner that they knew they had found their dog. They called her Chance and say she has 'enhanced every facet' of their lives.

I wanted the book to educate people about how animals end up in rescue pounds and what can be done to address these issues, and to encourage people to consider adopting an animal. I particularly wanted to share the mental health benefits of having a pet. We've had great feedback and the reviews have been amazing.

As well as the Sydney Dogs and Cats Home, I volunteer with Sydney Wildlife and with Wild2Free Kangaroo Sanctuary in the Mogo State Forest near Batemans Bay. My photos document the work they do while encouraging people not to be frightened of wild animals or feel the need to harm them.

Interestingly, I often find domestic animals more stressed at having their photos taken than wildlife, usually because they've been mistreated. When a wild animal is brought to the studio it's generally because they're injured or sick. My aim is to capture their personalities. Even snakes are very different from one another. Growing up in the bush, I was taught to be petrified of snakes. Breaking that fear has been a challenge – it does still kick in every now and then, particularly if the snake I am photographing is venomous.

My hardest assignment was when Wild2Free asked me to document wildlife in the sanctuary after the devastating bushfires in early 2020. It was incredibly, brutally sad. There were a few kangaroos, a few birds and millions of mosquitoes. I was fully dressed from head to toe, but the mosquitoes were biting through my clothes, and I think that's a sign that there was nothing for them to eat. I couldn't see, couldn't use my camera, and when I breathed, they would come into my mouth. It was like nothing I have ever experienced.

TURNING POINTS

As I was driving into the sanctuary, I saw a squashed death adder in the middle of the road. I thought, *You poor snake – you managed to survive this incredible, horrific fire and then you get run over by a car!* It struck me that I might easily have died myself when I was bulldozed by the claims assessor but, unlike the death adder, I survived and, in the process, found my purpose.

'Music gives me a language to express myself. I've always written what I thought was a true expression of who I am. I feel this incredible power when I write.'

Elena Kats-Chernin

Listening to the language of music

The minute I compose a piece of music or finish a project, I start thinking of other melodies, other harmonies. My brain never really stops. New melodies and ideas start creeping in to replace those that have gone. I do try to take a break, to watch something on television or read, but it's very hard. After a short time my brain starts moving back to music.

I knew from the time I was four that composing was more important to me than playing the piano. I was born in Tashkent, the capital city of Uzbekistan, in 1957. My father was an engineer and my mother was an eye surgeon. In 1961 they were sent to work in Yaroslavl, on the Volga River in Russia. It's a very old, very beautiful town. It was here my older sister, Larisa, started having piano lessons. I would sit and watch and when the teacher left, I played all the pieces Larisa had been learning. I just did it. The notes made sense to me much more than words. The language of music was just there.

My parents immediately arranged for me to have piano lessons. I used to get bored very quickly as I kept moving ahead with music. I played anything I saw. My mother was a fine pianist, so we had a lot of music at home. We had Chopin, Beethoven, Gounod, we had Schubert songs, Schumann songs, Rachmaninoff. I played everything

TURNING POINTS

and anything that came under my fingers and remember being so tiny my feet wouldn't touch the pedals. I had a pile of books, mostly music books, supporting my legs.

I was too young to go to school – you must be seven to start school in Russia – and I loved sitting at the piano not playing what someone else had written, just improvising. I realised that when I started improvising, that's when everybody went 'aha!' That was the eye-opener for my parents, that I could play something that nobody had composed. I played for hours. I would improvise, improvise, improvise.

I wrote *Lullaby* by accident. I don't know how it happened. I was five or six and they made me play it all the time, which was good because it solidified it in my head. I composed other pieces but can't remember them as well. *Lullaby* I revised many years later, when my youngest son, Nick, said he really liked it.

I was at home alone as my parents were working and Larisa was at school. One day I fell and cut my head open, and after that I was sent to school even though I was not yet seven. I loved school. I was eager to learn and loved being praised. I was always praised because I was such a goody-goody two shoes!

For the next eight years my days were divided between school, music lessons and figure skating. My friends would complain that I never had time for them, and it was true. After school I took a bus to my music teacher's place, and then another bus to the skating rink (my mother wanted us to be fit) and then another bus to the Sobinov Conservatory, where I studied musical theory, history, harmony and eventually composition. Every aspect of music had to be studied before I was allowed to compose, but I composed all the time anyway.

Today you see super-talented children on YouTube. It's a big deal and they are widely known. I was a child prodigy but nobody knew about me. Occasionally I played in a concert, and I won a lot of prizes in music competitions, but it wasn't my aim to be famous. I think fame is damaging. I was quite happy to be low-key. I was of course treated a bit differently, but I'm glad the attention I did receive didn't go to my head. I could have been this obnoxious, immature person, but I was very shy, always very shy. A late developer in many ways. I still am a little shy.

I had my first big turning point when I was fourteen and went on my own to Moscow. Russia has this very strict system of teaching music. The standard is extremely high. I felt I had gone as far as I could go with my music in Yaroslavl and decided to take the entry exam for the Gnessin State Musical College, the best in Russia. Six hundred students applied. I was one of fifteen or sixteen accepted.

The teachers at Gnessin were like gods – they wrote the textbooks we used. Our studies were very intense, very controlled. But within control there's always freedom. I learnt to make my own freedom. Now, always in my music, I set limits, because it gives me a framework. Then I open those borders and say, 'But I can work inside those limitations.'

Life at Gnessin was very basic, like in a camp. I shared a small room with three, sometimes four, other students. We had very few things and all wore the same clothes every day. We didn't have a washing machine. We were given 30 roubles a month (about $60 Australian in today's money), which was plenty to live on. We had to learn to cook, to be sociable. Suddenly I had friends who didn't think I was weird.

The hard part was just getting food. We sometimes stood in queues for up to three hours a day. We shared with each other a lot.

I only visited my family twice a year during my three years at Gnessin. Buying train tickets was so difficult. Every person waiting in the queue took at least twenty minutes because the process was all done by phone. The station staff were sitting on the phone, often not getting through. You could be there all day.

Even though I had excellent marks at Gnessin, my future career prospects were restricted because I was Jewish. Graduating students were allocated teaching posts throughout the Soviet Union, and although there was no overt antisemitism, I don't think I would have been offered the same opportunities as other students.

But everything changed in 1975, when we moved to Australia. My father's sister, Maya, had married a Polish man and they migrated to Sydney in 1965. My father's request to visit them was refused by the authorities, so he decided we would migrate too. It was the Brezhnev era and a good many Jewish intellectuals were able to leave Russia. I was excited as the wide world, the capitalist world, fascinated me. An ordinary person couldn't really travel outside of Russia, and I was interested in what lay beyond the borders.

I was accepted by the Sydney Conservatorium of Music and my first shock was having to choose my own subjects. As a child in Russia, we had people telling us what we could do, what we had to do, but the minute I got to the conservatorium they told me to choose my own subjects and I said, 'I don't know how to choose anything.' I found it very difficult. My second shock was being introduced to the photocopier and discovering I could copy my music for ten cents a sheet instead of writing it out by hand again and again and again. I thought it was the greatest invention in Australia.

At the conservatorium I studied composition and piano as a double major and was discovered by the late great composition teacher Richard Toop. He had been in Europe working with German composer Karlheinz Stockhausen and, shortly after his appointment and arrival at the conservatorium, he heard a piece I had composed for a student concert. I was playing the mouth organ while playing the piano with my left hand and another student was playing the oboe.

After the concert, Richard came up to me and said, 'Would you like to study composition with me?' This was a real honour. I became his first and only composition student in that year. Later he took on more individual students, but he was mainly lecturing in musicology and studies of new music.

I was very good at maths and logic. Even though my music seems to flow unchecked as from a fountain, I must be logical, I have to know the whole breadth of the piece and its structure. For my final exam at the conservatorium, I wrote my own concerto. I was clever enough to realise that if I wrote it myself I could play whatever I liked, which gave me the freedom to improvise half of it.

When I graduated in 1980, I was awarded a two-year German academic exchange scholarship to study with the composer Helmut Lachenmann in Hanover. It was here I met my husband. We had three sons, but it wasn't a good marriage. I had a husband who didn't earn much money and was incurring debts. I was desperate. When Nick was a baby I used to earn money by playing in a piano bar. The marriage didn't last.

There was no money in writing the sort of edgy, discordant, modernist music required by festivals, so I said to myself I had to do something else to earn a living. Fortunately I managed to find work as a theatre composer. This involved composing for drama theatre and ballets and took my music in a lighter direction. It also gave me the chance to work in an electronic studio and learn new techniques, which was exciting and fun.

I lived in Germany for thirteen years. The year I decided to come back to Australia, the Centre for Art and Media Technology in

TURNING POINTS

Karslruhe commissioned me to write a piece called *Clocks* for the Ensemble Modern.[22] It premiered on 7 November 1993. Thankfully it got recorded. It changed my life because that's the piece which opened doors.

Clocks premiered two months before I landed in Sydney with my three boys. It got Richard Tognetti, musical director of the Huntington Festival, interested, and then Barrie Kosky, director of the Adelaide Festival. It attracted international attention, as did *Cadences, Deviations and Scarlatti*, a commission from the Sydney Alpha Ensemble. In 1994, it was awarded the best composition by an Australian composer. I also received the Jean Bogan Prize for my piano piece *Charleston Noir*.

All this was a brilliant new beginning musically, but not financially. It was just individual performances of pieces, so I was still struggling. They were hard times. To make ends meet I decided to learn bookkeeping, and within two weeks of starting the course was offered a position teaching composition at the Sydney Conservatorium for a year. While I enjoyed teaching talented young minds, the lectures and their preparation took a huge amount of time and headspace and left very little time to compose.

Near the end of that year, a friend said to me, 'You've got to think about what you want to do and if it's composing, all the energies in the world will come and help you.' I also talked to my mother and sister and said, 'Will you support me if I don't renew the contract at the conservatorium and instead make a commitment to my own music? Will you support me if it doesn't work?' And they said, 'We will always feed you and your children.'

The boys and I moved into the empty house I had just bought while I still had the job at the conservatorium. I thought, *Oh my god, how am I going to survive?* But it was good. Every one of my sons had his

172

own room and I could play the piano all day long, all night long. I could work. I could be much freer with my music, and commissions started coming in.

Everything changed when my middle son got sick in October 1998. He went into a catatonic state at school and was admitted to hospital. He was diagnosed with schizophrenia and I became his carer.

I had a few commissions in the pipeline, one from the Australian Chamber Orchestra, one from Musica Viva and another for the soundtrack of a documentary film. It was hard to work on them because Alex sat with me in my music room and I had to think up tasks to keep him busy. He was often jumpy and his mood changed frequently. While it was challenging, it was more the grief and sadness that was difficult to live through. It was disruptive but I learnt to work through the disruption.

I have had many turning points in my life, but this was the big one. It completely changed me, changed my life, changed my attitude to composing. I decided I didn't want to write this edgy, discordant music anymore. It was better for my son when I wrote something soothing. He preferred it.

Alex getting sick was the most important event in my life because the life you know is no longer the life you're living and the life you think you're going to have is no longer there. It was the same for him. His life is so restricted now, I feel I have to compensate for that and make things as joyful, as calming, as possible for him. So I restrict my own life and really concentrate on my music. I've been given a gift and I've got to use it. I feel like that's my duty.

There's a Russian word, *yazyk*, that can mean language or speech, idiom or accent, even phraseology or tongue. Music is my *yazyk*. It gives me a language to express myself. I've always written what I thought was a true expression of who I am. I feel this incredible power when I write. I feel I can create anything.

Somewhere between 2005 and 2012, people started saying to me that my music was too soft, that it didn't have an edge, a climactic moment. That it didn't go anywhere. 'It's pleasant, people like it, but it doesn't give you a kick,' they said. I thought about that and started creating works like *Prelude* and *Cube*, works with lots of highs. Suddenly you have the choir with the big sound, suddenly you have something that sweeps you along, something that really fills your heart. I started thinking bigger. I had been writing lot of small pieces. I often say I am a miniaturist, I like small pieces, but for some time my commissions have become bigger projects requiring long phases of workshopping and orchestrating.

My Opera Australia commission to compose the music for the opera *Whiteley*, which tells the story of the Australian artist Brett Whiteley, was such a project. I wrote it three times, each time differently because I had a different attitude to it. The first version was a bit like a musical, the second a bit Kurt Weill and the third was much more trying to achieve a sound that reflects his art. The opera premiered in July 2019 and in February 2020 was shortlisted for the International Opera Awards.

In 2020 I composed a piece for the Sydney Philharmonic Choirs on different migration stories, *Human Waves*. It's about what Australia is made of, about diversity and the first impressions of different people. Tamara-Anna Cislowska wrote the libretto. She interviewed people she knew, like the father of one of her students. He had an amazing story of escaping from Vietnam.

I already have some ideas musically for a work and it's making my heart sing, which in turn is what makes my pen write. I sit at my piano, my pen in my hand, and put dots on paper. That's all it is, dots on paper, but of course the magic is organising them in a meaningful way.

'My idea was not just to tell an incredible story but to touch lives and help people understand.'

Yuot Ajang Alaak

Saving the lost boys of South Sudan

Coming to Australia from a refugee camp in Kenya when I was sixteen was the highlight of my life. That was when I truly believed I could take charge of my future.

But the biggest turning point was the day I got my father back. The date, 13 February 1989, will be forever etched in my memory. He had been jailed in North Sudan six years earlier and we were told he had been killed – but it wasn't true. He eventually escaped and found us – me; my mum; my little sister, Athok; and my half-brother, Bul – in the Pinyudo refugee camp in Ethiopia. Seeing Dad again, hugging him, crying with him, was like a resurrection. It was the day I truly began to believe in the power of God.

My dad, Ajang Alaak, was a Dinka from the village of Majak in South Sudan. He was a gifted child and the tribal elders sent him away to school. He eventually trained as a teacher. After the first Sudanese civil war, which ended in 1972, Malek Secondary was established in Bor Town, capital of Jonglei, his home state. Dad was appointed its first principal. It was 1978, the year I was born. Eventually Dad was made head of educational planning for South Sudan, overseeing the establishment of new schools throughout the country. He passionately believed that education was the only solution to the problems that his people and his country faced.

Tragically, the president of Sudan tore up the peace agreement between North and South Sudan in May 1983 and civil war broke out again. Troops were sent from the north to impose the Arabic language and sharia law on South Sudan, even though we were mostly Christian or animalist. Scores of people were killed. When the war broke out, Dad was trapped in Khartoum, in the north, where he had gone to organise supplies for southern schools. My mother, Preskilla, had to flee to Majak with me and Athok. We walked for days with the help of two of my uncles and when we arrived, we were welcomed by the entire village – most of whom were my relatives.

Apart from the constant anxiety about what was happening to my father, living in Majak was one of the happiest times of my life. It is a beautiful place, the landscape covered with acacia trees. There I was surrounded by family – grandparents, uncles and aunts, cousins – and growing up in a tranquil environment, free of disease, free of war, just living as one with nature. It was a peaceful, idyllic existence, one that millions of South Sudanese enjoyed before the war. It took me a while to adapt to village life, but I soon learned how to look after the goats in the mornings while Mum fetched the water. She milked the goats and cows at the end of the day and cooked a meal for us.

My uncles had a small handheld radio, which was our only window to the outside world. We listened every day, hoping to hear news of a peace deal, and I prayed for a ceasefire so that Dad could come home. One day in early March 1986, almost three years after the war had started, we heard news that Dad had been arrested by the government of Sudan and was in prison. He had ruffled a lot of feathers, emphasising education when the country was at war and everyone was talking guns, but people respected him highly for standing up for what he believed in, for being honest and incorruptible in a world full of corruption.

Five months after I heard that Dad was a political prisoner, the government broadcast the news that he had been killed. We mourned him in accordance with Dinka tradition: we had our heads shaved and wore animal-skin necklaces, and drums were beat as the family sang the spirit of my father into the afterlife. It was stressed that I, as Ajang's son, was to carry his legacy. I was only seven and felt the enormous burden of responsibility to protect Mum and Athok. For hours each day Athok and I sat with Mum, holding her hand as she wept.

One morning in late October, after I had let the goats out for their morning graze, I got back to the village to find the entire extended family gathered outside our hut. My uncle Pageer told us he had news, good news. He placed his hands on my shoulders and said, 'Yuot, your father is alive!'

Athok, Mum and I huddled together, sobbing uncontrollably.

Uncle Pageer went on, 'We've been told Ajang has been tortured and is now in prison in Malakal. But he is alive. He is not dead. God has brought him back to us.'

A year and a half went by, and people passing through our village warned us that the war was creeping closer to Majak. There were reports of fierce fighting spreading across the country. Thousands of South Sudanese were fleeing to neighbouring countries such as Ethiopia. My mother was in a very difficult position. She was the rock of our family. My book, *Father of the Lost Boys*, does not do enough justice to the women of South Sudan like my mum, who were not only mothers but, for long periods of time, fathers too. Mum was the glue, the gel, that kept us all together, who kept hope alive.

She had to take on the traditional role of the man of the house by finding food and safeguarding the animals. She also had to ensure we escaped the war.

Mum decided we had to leave Majak and make our way to Pinyudo, in Ethiopia, where we heard there was a refugee camp. It was hundreds of kilometres away, through arid land, savannah, dangerous forests, across crocodile-infested rivers – all with the constant threat of aerial bombardment, landmines and ambushes.

We left in March 1988. It took weeks to reach the safety of Pinyudo. Mum mostly walked and managed to persuade a South Sudanese soldier who had once been taught by my father to sneak me and my sister into an army truck occasionally. We would find each other at the end of the day. Mum was always exhausted. It only occurred to me when I started writing the book that there wasn't enough food for all of us and that after she fed us she often lay down hungry.

There were thousands of boys at Pinyudo with no parents, so my mum also became a mother to a lot of these boys, many of whom died of hunger and neglect. They were known as the lost boys. Mum and some other women talked with them, shared Bible stories, cooked for them. For the first time in their lives these boys started to feel the warmth of a mother's love – something they had missed for years and years. Most of them were aged between eight and twelve and had been sent to Pinyudo by their village elders to save them from the war. It was extremely hard at Pinyudo to keep us safe and fed, as men with guns ruled and were the only ones who were ever truly safe.

I was playing football with Bul one afternoon when Athok came running, calling us to come. Mum and some of our relatives were listening to a man speaking on the radio. It was Dad. For the first time I truly believed he was alive. He spoke about escaping to Ethiopia and said he had come to find his family and to work for the liberation of his people. Dad arrived at Pinyudo just over two weeks later, driven in an old Toyota truck. He was quickly surrounded by friends and relatives. Women danced and sang, and men ran in a circle round the vehicle, cheering. He was led to our hut, where Mum was waiting, and we all clung to him and each other, sobbing.

Our enemy in South Sudan was the government of Sudan, which was trying to change who we were. We had to take our future into our own hands – so it was a war of liberation. The British had sold us out and left us to our own devices. The government in the north took advantage of the situation and that's when the genocide happened. It cost millions of people their lives. The dictator of Ethiopia offered us protection and we were safe there in the camps, but he was facing challenges from Ethiopian rebels who were getting support from the Sudanese government. So Ethiopia became embroiled in its own civil war. The rebels promised to kick us out of Ethiopia when they seized power, and when the fighting crept closer to Pinyudo we had no choice but to prepare to leave.

Dad went into operational mode. He was determined to save the lost boys from becoming child soldiers, to somehow give them a future, an education. To him the pen is a more powerful weapon than the gun. He planned their departure meticulously with almost no resources. Having been Director of Planning in South Sudan before the war, planning was something he did well. He divided the lost boys into twelve groups of 1200. Each group had a leader and eight adults, as well as some caretakers, who distributed food and helped with discipline. Food supplies mostly came from the International Committee of the Red Cross, the United Nations and World Vision. Each boy was given a jerrycan to hold his food.

TURNING POINTS

We left Pinyudo early one morning in June 1991. Each group started half an hour after the one before. I was in Group 7. It was very organised. As soon as we stopped somewhere, runners were sent out to check on how the groups were going and whether their members had all survived. The aim was to get everyone to the Gilo River, near the border with South Sudan, as quickly as possible.

We walked through thick jungle inhabited by lions and hyenas. The whole jungle was alive with predators. By the time we reached the next stopping point in the morning, a truck would be waiting with beans and rice and the boys would sit and cook and fill their jerrycans and rest. My mother and sister were with the rest of the refugees and followed us at their own pace.

At Gilo, we were joined by thousands of unaccompanied minors from other Ethiopian refugee camps at Itang and Dimo, all terrified of the oncoming slaughter. Dad now had around 20,000 lost boys in his care. The river was swollen and infested with crocodiles, and Dad borrowed a dozen canoes from soldiers camping at Gilo. Each canoe carried about eleven boys at a time. The canoes went day and night, day and night. Sometimes they overturned. It was terrifying. Hundreds of boys lost their lives in the Gilo River.

The crossing took more than two weeks. The loss of so many boys was a low point for Dad, but in the sense that so many thousands were saved, the crossing was a huge success. If Dad's story was to happen today, I'm pretty sure it would've been covered live on the BBC and ABC. But those were different times.

We were heading for a town in South Sudan called Pochalla. By the time we got there, our food supplies had run out. No one in the world knew we were there. We were starving. When a small Red Cross plane came and landed near us, Dad begged them to help. They promised that food would come, and the next day a plane flew overhead. But to our horror, it came from the Sudanese airforce and dropped bombs, not food. Another plane came the day after, and this time it was the International Red Cross coming to assess the situation. Again, they promised us food. There was a great sense of urgency as we knew what the enemy was capable of.

Any hope we had of staying in South Sudan was soon gone when we heard that the nearest town to us had been captured and that thousands of mujahideen were marching towards us with their tanks and armoured vehicles. Dad got the news at six o'clock one evening and decided we had to leave immediately.

We walked all night and crossed the border into Kenya the next morning at a small town called Lokichogio. To make our way through South Sudan to Kenya was a miracle. We were not only fleeing Ethiopian rebels and the mujahideen and the National Islamic Front (the army of the government of Sudan), which had declared a jihad, we were escaping Islamic volunteers from places like Iraq in what was essentially a holy war fought between Islam and Christianity.

From Lokichogio we were moved to Kakuma, another small town, and were told, 'This will be your new home.' There was nothing much there, just a few trees. We were the first refugees to arrive. Kakuma is now one of the biggest refugee camps in the world, with about 180,000 refugees living there.

Quite often I hear people talk about how big the camps are getting, how facilities are improving, but for me the mere fact that they are there at all is itself a failure. It's when they don't exist, that's when we can say we've succeeded. My life in the village was peaceful and tranquil. That's what South Sudanese people remember, that's what they want to go back to. A refugee camp is like a prison. You're trapped unless you're among the lucky ones, like my family. Getting the chance to come to Australia in 1995 was like winning the lottery.

Even though South Sudan became an independent country in 2011, the situation there is bad. We have been through thirty years of war and do not have any of the skills of state building. We have one of the lowest literacy rates in the world; we have people in their forties, fifties and sixties who have never been to school. We have a country to run without the knowledge or the tools. The only thing our people know is how to fight, how to resist.

In Australia my father did everything he could to raise awareness about the camps and what was happening in South Sudan. He talked to schools, churches and charities. He spoke to the media. He even persuaded politician Philip Ruddock to go to Kakuma and meet with the lost boys and the many thousands of refugees there. Mum and Dad are devout Anglicans and due to Dad's efforts, the Synod of the Anglican Church of Australia passed a resolution acknowledging the persecution of the people of South Sudan and resolved to help. This led to thousands of South Sudanese refugees settling in Australia. Some returned home when South Sudan became independent, but most have stayed and built new lives. For many, it was a struggle to overcome the trauma they had experienced.

I am extremely proud of my father and want his story to be known. I suggested to him that he write a book, but we realised it was too hard for him, so I wrote it instead. It is my story too. It wasn't an easy undertaking with a full-time job and young children, but I just had to do it. Essentially Dad and I did it together. He read every page, every draft. He and Mum were my main reference points.

My idea was not just to tell an incredible story but to touch lives and help people understand what the lost boys had gone through. The lucky ones are living not only in Australia but in the United States, Canada and many European countries. The unlucky ones are still living in Camp Kakuma, including some of my relatives. I really feel vindicated for all the hard work I did on the book – that thousands of people are reading it and are touched by it.

'You need to cultivate the passion and drive to continue pursuing your goals despite the inevitable challenges that arise along the way.'

Siobhan Stagg

Appreciating the beauty of imperfection

My passion for, my interest in, music has always been there, but I didn't pursue it in a serious way until I was at university. I knew nothing about the European opera scene. I just knew that I loved singing and performing. As a child I used to record shows on television, like the gala concert for the Royal Children's Hospital Good Friday Appeal and *Carols by Candlelight*. I would watch them over and over again and try to sing like the singers on television. I was always singing around the house using a spoon as a microphone.

We lived in Mildura, in north-western Victoria, where my parents were both schoolteachers. They didn't have any experience with music, but were good, salt-of-the-earth people. They encouraged me and my two brothers to try lots of different sports in our spare time, but it wasn't until I found the music world in Mildura that I felt I was where I belonged.

It happened quite by chance when I was ten, almost eleven. My father and his brothers were planning my grandfather's funeral and knew that I loved singing. They said, 'Siobhan, would you like to stand in front of the microphone in the church and sing "Amazing Grace" and we'll all sing along with you?' I remember being very nervous but it felt like an honour to do that for my grandfather.

TURNING POINTS

An older second cousin of mine, Marcia Harrison, was there. She lived in Bairnsdale, quite a way from Mildura, so I didn't see her very often. As I left the church, she slipped an envelope into my hand. It contained a $100 note and a card that said: *This is to pay for your first singing lessons – and please invite me when you sing at the Sydney Opera House.*

This was a turning point for me as it compelled me to take my music more seriously. I started having half-hour singing lessons every week. The emphasis was not so much on classical music but on light popular music – musicals and showtunes. It was great. I loved it.

Living in a small country town had its advantages for a budding singer. I was called on to sing at every event there was, from school fetes to amateur musicals. I sang at everything – every eisteddfod, New Year's Eve concerts by the river, Christmas concert. And at church every weekend. I even sang in a rock band.

Even though I was singing so much in public, I never considered doing it professionally. It was just a hobby, as my parents kept saying. Not because they weren't supportive – they loved my singing – but in their world, education was the most important thing. They were both the first in their families to go to university and they encouraged us to aim for medicine or law. Both my brothers became doctors.

It wasn't until I was in Year 12 and went to an open day at the University of Melbourne that I discovered the conservatorium and realised you could study music. *This is what I am going to do,* I decided. *This is where I belong!* But, being sensible, I enrolled in a double degree in arts and music to keep my options open. They told us on the first day at the conservatorium that only an average of five per cent of us would make a living as performers, which was a shocking thing for a hall full of budding musicians to hear, but it was true.

Apart from starting piano lessons with the organist at church when I was fifteen, my formal training in classical music was relatively limited. I first heard a symphony orchestra in Melbourne when I was eighteen and was blown away. So, while I was behind the other students in terms of knowing the classical repertoire, I was ahead of them in terms of how many times I had stood up in front of a crowd and performed. It was invaluable experience.

During my first year at the University of Melbourne I lived at St Mary's, my mother's old college. Then I was offered a full residential scholarship at Trinity College, where I sang in the choir, doing a lot of small solos within the choral pieces. It was with that choir that I first went overseas and discovered that there is a big musical world out there beyond Australia.

I left university with great marks and a few small concert engagements but not really knowing what my next step was. I was living in a share house in Melbourne and doing casual work, such as waitressing, when I had a life-changing phone call from Amy Black of the Melba Opera Trust.[23] She said she'd been keeping an eye on me for some time and that the trust would like to offer me one of their inaugural singing scholarships. This floored me, as I had no idea I was being considered.

The Melba Opera Trust offers a unique program tailored to each scholarship recipient.[24] As Nellie Melba herself said, a beautiful voice is not enough. The staff at the Melba Opera Trust look at what you need, what your strengths and weaknesses are, and design a program around you. I learned public speaking, for example, how to dress and how to negotiate a contract.

A second phone call from Amy was to say that David Jones, the department store, had won an electric piano in an auction. They couldn't use it and wanted to give it to me to help my training. I was overwhelmed and thought, *Someone believes in me more than I believe in myself.*

I held the Amelia Joscelyne Memorial Scholarship for four years. It allowed me time and took away the financial pressure so that I could focus on my professional development. It enabled me to be ready when I applied for other scholarships, which took me overseas. And I was fortunate to win several, including the Australian International Opera Award and the Italian Opera Foundation Award.

After I left the Melba Opera Trust, I had another amazing life-changing break. In 2011 I was doing a summer school in Graz, Austria, on a scholarship from the Opera Foundation for Young Australians when I was approached by Clemens Klug, an agent. He told me he wanted to work with me and set up a series of auditions for me around Europe. It was through Clemens that I was taken into the Salzburg Festival's young artist program and then joined the Deutsche Oper Berlin as a young artist in 2013. These were the first international professional engagements of my career. I was twenty-five.

I worked with Clemens for six years and he helped open many doors. One of the most unexpected and exciting happened in January 2015. I was standing in the boarding queue at Tegel Airport, about to fly to Zurich for an audition, when my phone rang. It was Clemens. Did I know the Brahms Requiem? Could I sing it this week with the Berlin Philharmonic and the award-winning conductor Christian Thielemann?

I couldn't believe what I was hearing. This was the holy grail of gigs. I said yes, I've done it before, but I need to know right now, before I board the plane.

'Give me two minutes,' Clemens said.

I let everyone pass me in the queue and he called me back and said, 'You're on!' I left the airport, got in a taxi and went straight to the

Berliner Philharmonic, where I found myself having a rehearsal with the orchestra immediately.

The concerts were sold out. Placido Domingo was in the audience. Angela Merkel was in the audience. Suddenly I was catapulted to another level.

The shortest time I've ever spent learning a role is five days. It was the title role in *Orpheus* by Luigi Rossi for the Royal Opera House in London, in collaboration with Shakespeare's Globe Theatre. Five days before the premiere, the main soprano got laryngitis. It's quite an obscure role, and the producers couldn't find anyone who knew it. I agreed to step in even though I had never heard it before. They emailed me a PDF of the score, flew me to London and I sang the first six performances. You can only do that in exceptional circumstances because that level of adrenaline is not healthy over long periods. I try to allow a year to build a new role into my bones slowly.

I don't read reviews. I agree with the late great American soprano Jessye Norman when she said she didn't *need* that kind of feedback, that singers know immediately on any given night if they've achieved what they wanted to achieve. The desperate hunt for affirmation in reviews can be dangerous for artists. A review can lift your spirits – or crush them in a moment. It's nice to read glowing reviews, but if someone writes something negative it's like poison: it stays in you, and you forget every positive thing that anyone ever said to you. I think it's wiser to build an honest and knowledgeable support network of people around you who can offer constructive feedback in a helpful way.

In her book *Grit* (2016), American psychologist Angela Duckworth writes that perseverance and resilience are more important than talent. I really resonate with that idea. I don't think I'm doing this as a living because I've got the most beautiful voice. The truth is, no matter how good you are, some people will connect immediately with your voice and some people won't. But I do think that growing up in Mildura instilled in me some sense of this grit, this determination to never give up. You need to cultivate the passion and drive to continue pursuing your goals despite the inevitable challenges that arise along the way.

One of the biggest challenges is handling performance psychology and dealing with anxiety. I always say to young singers when they ask me about coping with nerves that you should give as much importance to your mental wellbeing and your psychological state as you do to the technical practice of singing scales and learning songs, because you can't have one without the other. It's very important to get the right amount of sleep and to have as healthy a lifestyle as possible. And then you must have people in your life you can trust. Really important for me was confiding in other singers I admired and hearing that everybody, however well known, still suffered from some level of stage fright and wondered whether they were good enough.

It's a great privilege to work full-time as an artist. When I think of my purpose as a singer, I am reminded of what American soprano Nadine Sierra once said: that the purpose of our job as singers is to showcase the beauty of imperfection. I love that – it's really freeing mentally because we can't be perfect all the time. In fact, I find that as a member of the audience, sometimes the most beautiful, touching, unforgettable moments aren't the perfect moments, they're when someone displays a moment of fragility or something indescribable that really touches you.

My base is Berlin, where I live with my husband, Nelson. Like my parents, we met at the University of Melbourne, so we've known each other a long time. I'm glad he knew me before I became successful. I think that starting relationships is hard for colleagues who are travelling all the time. Nelson and I joke that maybe it's easier to maintain a happy marriage when you see each other as seldom as we do. I spend many nights alone in a hotel room studying the score for the next performance. Luckily, I love languages. At university I studied phonetics and Italian, a language which for me is a joy. I am now also very comfortable in German and French.

Being good at languages in crucial. A singer must understand every word of an opera to portray the right emotion. We're basically actors, so we need to be able to think each word as if it were our own language. This gives the sound intention and the audience engages with that. When a singer doesn't understand the words, their singing lacks something.

Did I ever get to sing in the Sydney Opera House? You bet. One of the most cherished experiences of my career was singing with the star tenor Roberto Alagna there in July 2016. We sang 'Caro elisir, sei mio' from *L'elisir d'amore*, by the Italian composer Gaetano Donizetti, as well as old favourites like 'Santa Lucia', 'O sole mio' and 'O mio babbino caro'. It was fun and the audience loved it – especially one person, for whom I had arranged the best ticket I could find: my cousin Marcia. It was some eighteen years after she had slipped me that card. When I think back to that day, I wonder who I would be if this hadn't happened. I certainly wouldn't be the me that I know.

'You must believe in your purpose 100 per cent – because if you don't, the struggle will defeat you and you'll give it away.'

Margaret Leggatt

Changing the landscape of mental health

My first experience working with people with mental illness was after I trained as an occupational therapist in the 1950s, then worked in psychiatric hospitals for eighteen months here in Melbourne and overseas in Canada. Some years later, after I was married with three sons, I wanted to get back to my profession and do something to complement my role as a wife and mother. I found a job as an occupational therapist at the Malvern Community Mental Health Centre.

It was the 1970s and the big mental institutions in Melbourne's psychopolis were being shut down. I became very conscious that many of the patients I was working with at the Malvern clinic would previously have been locked up for life. In theory, they were being helped to live in the community, but they were being looked after by their mothers and fathers. Given that parents were being blamed for causing schizophrenia in their sons and daughters, then blamed for not managing appropriately, their burden was intolerable.

The psychiatric superintendent at Malvern suggested I do some research into families coping with severely ill sons and daughters, so I enrolled in a master's degree at Monash University. I decided that I would find a group of families in the eastern suburbs of Melbourne

TURNING POINTS

and work with them over a fairly long period of three to four years and document everything that happened in their lives.

It took quite some time to find families who were prepared to talk to me, so damaged had they been by the blaming and shaming they had already experienced. But it did not take long for me to be very moved by the devotion, the resilience, the passionate care that these parents gave to their mentally ill sons and daughters. This was the beginning of my profound respect for families who care for those with schizophrenia.

I found it hard to believe that these families were being blamed for causing mental illness in their children. This view came from the results of some very questionable research by people like R.D. Laing, a Scottish psychiatrist who had a very mad mother. He was one of the theorists who said we don't have to look very far for the cause of schizophrenia, it's these terrible parents. There was a lot of very questionable research based on ridiculous hypotheses and 'proven' with very small samples that has now, thank God, been totally discredited.

After two years of following the lives of these families, I was totally, totally stressed. I was identifying with parents with late-teenage, young-adult children, and wondered how I could cope if one of my own children developed a mental illness. I was dealing with some catastrophic situations, such as the mother who told me she had a gun hidden in the bottom of her wardrobe, that she didn't feel she could cope with her son much longer and was prepared to shoot him and herself. I'm supposed to be an objective researcher – to not get personally involved – but what do you do with information that could point to murder and suicide?

The stress became intolerable. I had to give up the work I was doing because I felt I was not coping emotionally, and this was impacting badly on my husband and children. I spent the next year working at the Lincoln Institute as a senior lecturer in occupational therapy. It was a terrible year. I got totally fed up with the infighting between well-educated people with jobs and careers and thought to myself, *There are people out there in far, far worse situations than privileged professionals.*

That break from the families I was working with enabled me to reflect on the situation without stress, although I continued to be haunted by what they were coping with. I reached a point where I knew I had to go back, that that's where my true commitment lay. I felt I had let the families down by walking away, but I also realised I couldn't allow myself to be so affected by the disastrous situations some were coping with. It didn't help them, and it certainly didn't help me.

At the end of that year away, I picked up my research with the families again. My master's became a PhD, but I was reluctant to write it up. Although I knew it was groundbreaking, I thought, *What's the point? It's all theory. I've actually got to do something practical with it.* I heard that the psychiatric superintendent and the social worker at the Malvern Community Mental Health Centre were planning to call a meeting of families to talk about what could be done by way of help and support for them, and I joined forces with them.

We advertised in the local press and around the clinic, but because the stigma associated with mental illness was so great, we thought we would only get between ten and twenty people. Well, 130 turned up! A group of us got together afterwards, sat round my dining-room table and divided people into geographic areas. This was how the first eleven support groups were formed.

We then went on to establish a formal organisation we called the Schizophrenia Fellowship of Victoria. I took the role of director; a neighbour offered to do our typing; my husband, Tom, did the legal work; and John O'Meara, a retired school principal and father of a severely mentally ill daughter, became president. One psychiatrist rang me and asked me what the hell I thought I was doing. 'You can't call something "schizophrenia"!' he said. I told him we can, and we will, and we did.

We worked from my dining room for about eighteen months without any funds at all and eventually got $20,000 from the government, which enabled us to rent a place in Collingwood. People came in huge numbers; it was quite overwhelming. This was the first time there was somewhere desperate families could go where people would listen. Then I started getting families who were prepared to talk to other families, and more support groups were formed. I think we eventually had thirty-three support groups around Victoria.

In my research I had done a lot of work studying what families need. Most of all they needed information to gain some understanding of the illness. Then they needed techniques to manage it. This was a big issue, because often the kids were seen as behaving badly and were punished rather than being treated for an illness.

I think the most effective thing we did was to put people in touch with one another via the groups. They learned from one another about how to manage. This was not only mutually supportive; it also helped get rid of the blame, shame and guilt that families were feeling. It was so terribly, terribly unfair that so little was happening for the families and for the young people with mental illness who were trying to cope with an unresponsive and punitive society.

After working at the Fellowship for about six or so years, I was again stretched to the limit. We were trying to do everything from helping other states set up their own fellowships – which involved a great deal of travel – to supporting families, developing housing and employment projects, and constant advocacy towards the destigmatisation of mental illness. There was so much to do I started having heart pain and was referred to a cardiologist, who warned me I could be heading for a heart attack. I was told that either I had to change my attitude to my work and cope without getting stressed or leave.

I changed my approach. I employed Jim Webb, who had been the warden at the University of Melbourne and had had a distinguished career in organisational (including non-government) development, to look at the work I was doing and tell me what he thought. His advice was to separate advocacy about mental illness from the grassroots support work. 'I think you need to develop another organisation to carry out advocacy and this needs to be done nationally,' he said. I was shocked. *What? Start another organisation when I can't cope with just the one?*

But I began canvassing support for a national organisation and was incredibly lucky to get Sir Edward Woodward on board. He was hugely famous: made a judge at forty-three, head of the Australian Security Intelligence Organisation and a prominent royal commissioner, including for the Royal Commission into Aboriginal Land Rights in the Northern Territory, which became known as the Woodward Royal Commission. He confessed to being almost totally ignorant about mental illness but agreed to accept the position if I felt that his name could be of use. It was. I was able to get ten or twelve very high-profile people involved, including journalist Anne Deveson, whose son had schizophrenia and had died.

The treasurer and board members raised $75,000, which kept the organisation afloat in its early years. That's how SANE (originally an acronym for 'Schizophrenia – A National Emergency', copied from the organisation in the United Kingdom) started. For a crazy period of some few years I was the paid director of the Schizophrenia Fellowship and the unpaid director of SANE.

Looking back, I can see that my unhappy year at the Lincoln Institute showed me where my true passion lay. It took me back into the mental health sector and I never again wavered in my belief in what I was doing. You must believe in your purpose 100 per cent – because if you don't, the struggle will defeat you and you'll give it away.

One of the biggest changes I have seen over the years is that so many people in the public eye now talk openly about their struggle with mental illness. I still have serious concerns for families caring for severely mentally ill young-adult offspring and lacking community support and in particular residential care. It's an issue my friend – poet and author Sandy Jeffs, who suffers from schizophrenia – and I explore in our book *Out of the Madhouse: From Asylums to Caring Community* (2020). We ask what has been lost and what has been gained by closing the big mental hospitals. What we found was that the closure of asylums created a raft of social problems that impact not only those with a mental illness but also those who live with them in the community.

The support services that were meant to replace institutions just haven't materialised and more people are ending up homeless or in jail. The long-term mentally ill have the lowest priority in our society, and we need to change that.

'As a teacher, I make a difference …
Ideally all teachers, not just good ones, can change a young person's life and help them reach their potential despite their circumstances.'

Gia-Yen Luong

Doing education differently

Ever since I was a teenager, my dream was to become a lawyer. Until my fourth year at university, I was quite adamant that that was what I would do. The reason was that I wanted to be able to help people who really needed to be helped in our society, and I was quite convinced that the law was the best way to do that. Wanting to give back, especially here in Adelaide, is important to us as a family, as my parents both came here as boat people and were made welcome.

My mother, Huong Tran, trekked through the jungle from Vietnam to Cambodia with her sister and then sailed to Thailand in a tiny fishing boat. They lived in Thailand in a refugee camp for some time. They had lost touch with their other siblings, but miraculously found them again and were eventually offered asylum in Australia. My father, Trung Luong, escaped from prison in Vietnam and left the country by sailing a boat into international waters, where he was rescued and brought to a refugee camp in Singapore. He too sought asylum in Australia. My parents met in Adelaide, married in 1993 and built a new life here, my dad as a self-employed builder, my mother as a nurse.

Listening to my parents tell their stories and understanding where they came from helps me appreciate their work ethic and their need to give back. They do a lot of volunteer work, especially in the Catholic community. It also helps me understand what drives me too. Mum works in a hospital and her friends there constantly ask her what she feeds her five kids that makes them so smart. 'What is the secret?' they want to know. One of my brothers has a great job as a mechanic at Mercedes-Benz, two of them are studying at the University of South Australia and the youngest is doing well at high school. Mum doesn't know how to respond because she just did what she felt was right. I've thought about it a lot. There must have been something in my parents that they were brave enough to leave Vietnam the way they did. They literally risked their lives. They are deeply grateful to Australia for taking them in and giving them so many opportunities.

I always found school easy. Mum and Dad took it for granted that my four brothers and I would take our studies seriously. I enjoy learning new things and reading, so my parents pushed me to do that. They set me up for success. They always encouraged me and my siblings to just do what we really, really liked and be good at it.

I didn't realise I wasn't the smartest person in the world until I enrolled in a five-year double degree in law and international relations at the University of New South Wales. UNSW Law School is quite selective about who it takes, which meant that all the other people in my cohort were top students from their schools. I found myself academically challenged for the first time. It was great. I loved my legal studies but found international relations too theoretical and switched to neuroscience, both for fun and because it's the science field I think we know least about. There's so much scope for asking really hard questions because we've done so well in other areas.

To supplement my scholarship allowance, I coached students from primary-school age to Year 12. They mostly came via a tutoring agency. Initially I also took a few university students, but after a while dropped them off because I found I liked working with the younger ones better. I was working a lot and just got to a stage where I realised that the most rewarding part of my day was the time I spent with my students. This was my turning point – coming to the realisation that it was teaching, not the law, that inspired me.

When you tutor privately, there are two buckets of students. One holds the students who are already getting an average of 80 or 90, and the other holds kids who are failing. It was working with students who were failing that I found most rewarding – students like Sophie, who, at Year 3, couldn't read. She wasn't stupid or naughty, she simply couldn't read. Her parents didn't know what to do. I worked intensively with Sophie for about a year to improve her recognition of and confidence with sight words as a way to get quick gains in her reading ability. Once she was feeling more confident with the decoding of texts, we moved on to comprehensive skills. I believe it was the extra time and practice that I was able to provide on a one-on-one basis in addition to her school support that helped her to catch up with her peers. She now reads well, and her spelling is incredible. Her entire approach to school has changed.

I was in my fourth year at university when I decided that I would become a teacher once I finished my degree. It caused quite a stir at college, but my parents accepted my decision completely. They were never really invested in me becoming a lawyer, but rather in me finding a career that would suit me and that I would find rewarding.

I looked for the most rigorous teaching course I could find and applied to join the Leadership Development Program run by Teach for Australia, an organisation aimed at closing the achievement gap between students from high and low socioeconomic areas.[25] I found myself training with others of a similar mindset, often trying to tackle the problem from different angles, which was really, really good. The course involved doing a Master of Teaching, and as part of this I was sent to teach maths and science to Years 7, 8 and 9 in a school in a low-socioeconomic area on the outskirts of Darwin, in the Northern Territory. A lot of teachers avoid these year levels like the plague, but I fit in well with them. I think I have a particular strength working with kids in this age group.

It was a tough school to teach in. It had a big mix of kids, including local Indigenous town kids and a few bush kids who came and went, kids from Defence Force families and others who had grown up in Darwin or on local farms. There were also a number of kids from migrant families. I had to learn quickly where my boundaries were and keep to them strongly. I'm quite a strong personality in the classroom and I always found that behaviour management was easier when my boundaries were clear.

When I first meet a child, I try to figure out where I stand with them and how best to take that child where he or she needs to be. It's like a puzzle. It takes a lot of emotional energy, especially with a big class. That's what I think about a lot, what to do with so and so, how I can better include them or better engage them. The biggest challenge when began teaching in the Northern Territory was trying to understand the kids' context and what the barriers were for them. The reasons kids mostly disengage or misbehave in class is because the work's too hard or not hard enough or they're not interested. Really, really good planning helps work out where the kids are at and helps the teacher to challenge the ones who are ready to be challenged and support the ones who aren't. When I had that figured out, I found my classes worked well and I didn't need to manage behaviour as much.

In the Northern Territory and afterwards, at the state high school in Adelaide where I taught for two terms, I developed an approach to teaching that was demanding both of the teacher and the students. I have no time for classes that involve watching a video or reading a text and answering questions. This is not true learning. It's lazy teaching. When I start a new unit, instead of just taking what's there, I reimagine the way it could be taught, and I just do it. I just do it differently.

I knew when I applied to Teach for Australia that I had found my purpose. I didn't expect to expand that purpose into making a difference in the quality of education in state schools in Australia. I believe the current system does not serve teachers or students. What is needed is a higher Australian Tertiary Admission Rank for people entering the teaching profession, more rigorous teacher training, better pay and greater respect for teachers in the community.

For some years – well before I started teaching – I had been thinking of applying for a Rhodes Scholarship when I left UNSW. Initially I saw this as a goal in itself, but while I was teaching in the Northern Territory I began to see it as a means to an end. By studying a Master of Science in Comparative and International Education at Oxford, followed by a PhD in Education, I would be able to return to Australia better equipped to bring about change in education policy and teaching.

I almost didn't apply for the Rhodes Scholarship because at that point in my career I didn't want to seek prestige for the sake of it if I could spend the time in the classroom. Going to Oxford for four years would detract from that and probably put me on a different professional trajectory, so it took a lot of reconciling. Ultimately, though, I want to have the biggest impact on education I can, and I thought the backing of the scholarship community would be a huge advantage for me.

TURNING POINTS

When I applied for the scholarship, I spelled this out clearly in my personal statement:

> As a teacher, I make a difference. However, in the long term I want to – need to – make a broader impact. Ideally all teachers, not just good ones, can change a young person's life and help them reach their potential despite their circumstances. Ideally, all schools, not just good schools, effectively serve their communities by shaping young people into leaders. This is not yet the case here in Australia.

In 2018, I was awarded a scholarship. I don't see the Rhodes Scholarship as another turning point but rather as a stepping stone. My dream is to use my growing expertise both in the classroom and in my studies to realise my vision of an equitable, and equitably successful, education system to give our young people what they deserve.

Teaching is not a highly regarded profession in Australia, it's not a field that attracts young achievers, and I'd like to see that change. I'd also like to see change in the way that we talk about how we measure achievement. Above all, I think how we train teachers and how we teach kids needs to be more rigorous. If you hold the teacher to a high standard, it means that what the students are taught is also of a high standard. Unfortunately, a lot of schools are run like businesses and the focus of school management is not always on the quality of teaching and learning. They're more concerned about what it looks like to an outsider. I feel teaching practice could be improved even in small ways, such as how a room is set up and how we greet the students.

I got married in August 2019, a few weeks before leaving for Oxford. In March 2020, the pandemic really took off in England. Oxford moved classes online and waived its residency requirement for all students. Luckily I had already completed the taught components of my course and was set to begin the research and writing for my dissertation. I could do this from home and so my husband and I decided to return to Australia. We just made it before the borders were closed to international returns.

I completed my dissertation at home in the first three months of my son's life and earned a distinction for it and for the degree overall. I'd have been lost without my husband because he reminded me to stay focused on my goal, my purpose. He believes I have a lot to give the world and especially to young people. He sees my care and compassion for kids and thinks I can bring about policy change.

At this stage I have no idea how that will happen or what it will look like. It could mean working in schools, in the public service, in politics – maybe working with Teach for Australia, or maybe with another organisation entirely. What I do know is that I am on my way and I believe that doors will open.

'As a food writer, I see myself as having an important role to play. So many people are disconnected from the land where the food they eat comes from.'

Richard Cornish

Living from farm to table

I haven't always been a food writer. I started working in television straight out of school. I grew up on a 150-acre dairy farm on the rich, fertile basalt slopes overlooking Western Port Bay on the Mornington Peninsula. It was idyllic country but, for me at the time, a cultural and economic desert. Most people were white and those who weren't were 'the other'. The school I went to, Peninsula Grammar, was the type of place where aspirational parents would send their kids. There was this constant niggling, grinding feeling, almost a tectonic thing, of people rubbing up against each other constantly, asserting their status.

Mine was a strong matriarchal family. My dad died when I was eight and Mum brought up the family – me, my brothers Roger and John and my sister, Georgina – on the farm by herself. At family functions there were these strong women born in the late nineteenth century who did everything. Auntie Zoe, for example, helped found the Collingwood Children's Kindergarten and agitated against the use of lead in cars because she'd seen the detrimental effect it was having on children's intelligence.

I finished Year 12 in 1984, did well, got into Arts at the University of Melbourne – then panicked. Because of complicated financial reasons relating to the burden of paying double probate owing to the early deaths of my father and grandfather, the farm had to be sold. It was a difficult time. I was the first in my family to be offered a place at university, but I was quite immature. I was a six-foot-two baby who felt lost. I found the enrolment process at university quite overwhelming and, looking at all the other young people there, I didn't feel I was qualified to attend. The imposter syndrome, perhaps. Nor did I know how I was going to pay for accommodation. I deferred.

Looking back, I can see that this was a major turning point in my life. I was scared. I didn't know what to do. I didn't see myself staying on in the Mornington Peninsula, so rather than venture into a world I didn't know, I decided to look for work in television because I had family contacts. Being immersed in TV from an early age, it was a culture I understood. I knew how it should look and sound and I had an idea of how it worked behind the scenes.

I found a job working for a small production company making a kids' television show for SBS called *Not Suitable for Adults*. It was marvellous. I painted sets and swept floors. I thrived. I really enjoyed the energy of being part of a team. Within six months I was working at Channel Nine, starting in the mailroom and ending up making TV shows. I never went back to uni. I sometimes regret it but recently, on a walk with my former English teacher, he said, 'Thank god you didn't go to university. It would have crushed your creativity!'

Live television was exciting. Any mistakes would be seen by millions of people. And I made them. There was a lot of pressure and you really learned from that. But then something started happening – something changed. It was the introduction of reality television. Networks realised they could make prime-time content a lot cheaper with shows like *Big Brother*.

This was the movement that created Donald Trump. He was a failing businessman until television producers got hold of him. He's actually a television construct. The people cynical enough to do that were the sort of people I was coming up against, whose values I didn't share, who treated people as objects. It was soul-destroying.

The defining moment for me in choosing to give up my career as a television producer was when my daughter Ginger was a baby. Once, when she was about six months old, I was producing a show. I started in the morning working on an edit, trying to fix other people's problems, and was still there at lunchtime the next day. I said to myself, 'I can't do this anymore. I have a wife and baby at home. If this is what is expected of me, it's ridiculous. I just can't do it.' I handed in my resignation the next day.

While I was working in television, I had started to write about food, probably to get back to those 150 acres by the sea, that rich soil, the grass and the cows. Leaving television meant making the change from wanting to write about food to making it a career. We didn't have a mortgage at that time. My partner Tiffany's dress design business was going well, which meant I could just go for it. I felt liberated. I was let loose to explore the world of food. I could take myself to a place that was full of stories.

Food is stories. If you look at a Christmas pudding recipe from Britain, for example, it takes you back to the Middle Ages. That's as far back as the Norman conquest in 1066! Making Christmas puddings represents an unbroken line of 1000 years. Here in Victoria, we have the eel story from the Gunditjmara people in Western Victoria that goes far further back in time – 6600 years.

Writing about food has led me in all sorts of different directions, but the most transformational has been encountering a tiny fraction of Indigenous culture. It made me see the world completely differently and freed me from the emotional baggage of a colonial upbringing. For Aboriginal peoples, food is basically one part of a matrix of stories – of life, of ancestry, of land, of art, of painting, stories, dance. It's all one. We tend to break things up into bite-sized portions that we can study, whereas the Indigenous understanding is holistic. Where we see our history as being linear with a thread trailing behind us, Indigenous peoples see the past, present and future as part of one continuum. I learnt this through twenty-five years of conversations about eels with the Gunditjmara people at Lake Condah in Western Victoria. Seventy kilometres northeast of Portland, Lake Condah was formed when Budj Bim – renamed Mount Eccles by nineteenth-century colonisers – erupted over 30,000 years ago.[26] The lava flow changed the course of creeks and rivers, forming a rocky landscape with the lake as part of a network of pools, canals and channels. The Gunditjmara people developed this 6600 years ago into a massive aquacultural system of weirs, dams and traps, where eels were raised, harvested, smoked and sent off for trade around the country for millennia.

I see food as another pathway that Indigenous peoples are using to educate us post-colonials to give us an insight into the way they see the universe. Their dances do this, their music does this. I believe food is beginning to do it too. It's a beautiful process, and I think the great healing of Australia will be the development of that understanding – bit by bit, bite by bite, mouthful by mouthful.

That's what I like about writing about food: it tells a bigger story. For me, food is a way into exploring the world. Food is not a destination, it's just a way of getting to a more informed place of understanding. Food is a constant line of human existence. If you start a conversation with food, you can go anywhere in the world, you can go anywhere in time, you can go anywhere in politics. If you wrap yourself in food and conversation, you can find out so much more about a person's background, their life experience and family than you could if you tackled it from any other point of view. Writing about food is ethnographic. You start with the soil, with the planting, the animals, and stories around those. Then it's about what and how people grow food and stories around that, how people cook food and the stories around that, how they preserve food and stories around that. So food writing is about carefully following the narrative of the complexity of how the food people eat came to be.

Food is not just about consumption. That's a completely reductionist way of looking at it. The way we talk about restaurants and the way we describe food is about a completely self-centred experience, especially if we just talk about how food tastes. The reason why it tastes as it does is because there are all these human micro decisions that makes food what it is. This includes the way humans interact with the natural environment, something the French encapsulate in their concept of *terroir*. That to me is amazing. Wine's the same. How many different decisions did that winemaker make? How many different decisions did the vigneron make to make that wine taste the way it does?

That's the most extraordinary thing about it. We have thousands of years of an unbroken lineage of food production. That's why there's such sadness about industrial food. It's smashed these connections, all these nexuses between people and land, people and soil, people and history, people and their ancestors. They've been broken by fast food!

As a food writer, I see myself as having an important role to play. So many people are disconnected from the land where the food they eat comes from. Ninety per cent of Australians live in the city and most of them don't understand the relationship between the food they eat and where it comes from. My role is to tell people what's going on and to completely, unabashedly, use the enticement and temptation of food and flavours to tell a different story – a story of country, culture and cuisine. For without food, nourishing food, we all die, both body and soul.

'I passionately believe that language and literacy are linked to human rights and equity.'

Rosalie Martin

Connecting hearts and minds

I learnt at a very early age what a disadvantage it is to struggle with communication. My older brother has a hearing impairment, and I could see how hard it was for him as a child and how hard it was for Mum to manage that. An incident at primary school when I was six brought this home to me in a shocking way. Sometimes my brother and I were in the same class, and on one occasion I watched him mercilessly bullied by a teacher who stood him up in front of all the kids and yelled at him for not responding to a question, despite knowing he was deaf. 'Why don't you answer?' he shouted at my brother. 'Are you deaf or something?'

I was horrified and angry with the teacher and felt helpless, but I believe this experience lit the flame that fuels my passion to help people with low-level language issues. I couldn't have articulated it when I was young, but I feel my life has always centred on questions of how we connect and communicate. I remember being aware even at six that if we could just be kind to each other, we would live in a world that didn't have the same degree of strife.

I grew up on a farm in South Australia and after leaving school applied to study speech pathology at Flinders University in Adelaide. I didn't get in the first year – they only took twenty-two students – so

TURNING POINTS

I did a year of science then applied for the course again the following year and was accepted as a mature-aged student. I was eighteen! It's an intense course that some do in two parts – a first degree, perhaps in psychology, followed by a two-year Master of Speech Pathology.

I think the profession is poorly named because it suggests that we're just looking at speech itself, that is, the production and mechanics of speech, whereas the work is the entire scope of human communication. As a speech pathologist, my life centres on questions of how we connect and communicate, our body language and tone of voice, the way we might use manners, the way we greet each other. Our training is in language, its normal development and its impaired development, and its structure and social use.

Many members of our community cannot read and write well enough to navigate the activities of daily life. They cannot read the street signs or fill in forms at the doctor's surgery. They don't understand the information on the electoral enrolment form and are unable to complete the census. They don't know which bottle is shampoo and which is conditioner; cannot read the menu in a café or the labels on pill bottles; don't understand the bus timetable; and ignore important letters and notices. Too often they feel stupid, their self-esteem around their ankles. Their vocabularies are weak and they can't express themselves. They often get frustrated and end up taking an oppositional stance towards authority. Or they passively withdraw and make themselves small. They might wear themselves out in hard-labour jobs, which are the only jobs they can get – if they get a job at all. Or they drift into a life of crime.

After graduating, I met Rich in Adelaide. We married and moved to Hobart, in Tasmania, where my two sons were born. I set up a private practice but only worked part-time while the boys were young. My strength as a speech pathologist, I believe, lies in the many-layered approach I developed in my clinic, especially in my work with children with autism spectrum disorder and those with severe literacy disorders. I understood the importance of listening, of empathising, of reading body language and of hearing what is unspoken. With children, above all, it was about making the work fun. I had to make it entirely joyful for them or else they would dig their little heels in. If children sense failure, they shut down.

I enjoyed the private practice model in my clinic, working with beautiful families in a beautiful team, yet I always had that burning within that we weren't meeting the needs of the many people who couldn't afford our service or for whom it was inaccessible, such as prisoners and the homeless. It was unrealistic, however, to put prices down in my clinic, as I had to pay my professional staff and keep them trained at a high level. So I decided to set up a charity I called Chatter Matters to offer speech pathology free of charge to those who badly needed help. This was in 2012, a year before the commencement of the National Disability Insurance Scheme, which has now created a lot of extra demand and ironically contributed to the increased awareness of the shortage of speech pathologists across the country.

When I look back, I realise I was a bit naïve to think I could meet all these needs, and yet I had also reached a stage where I could see that if I continued to work one-on-one across a little table with individuals, it would be great for them but wouldn't be influencing the systems that we were working within.

Soon after I started Chatter Matters, I realised that I didn't really know how to use the charity effectively. I needed different networks, different skills. I did the Tasmanian Leaders Program specifically for that reason. It was a transformational course. It gave me access to many people who were movers and shakers, who had their hands on levers of power. These were people who understood how the system works and who enabled me to understand that what I was seeking to do was to bring my insights, knowledge and voice to supporting, activating and stimulating systems-based change on a wider scale than working with individuals across a tabletop. By the end of the year, I had the contacts I needed.

One of the things we did in the Tasmanian Leaders Program was visit Hobart's Risdon Prison. It was the first time I had ever been to a prison and was especially interesting for me as I had been thinking for some time about the impact of child speech and language disorders in creating disadvantage in adult lives. When we moved to Hobart, before starting my clinic I had worked with children in a community health centre in a low-socioeconomic area. After I left that job, I often thought about the children in that area who had no access to therapy or who struggled to communicate – like my brother. Communication and learning difficulties that mean students can't understand their teacher or can't contribute in class may lead to challenges in behaviour. I wrote about this in *The Hobart Mercury*: '[These children] may act up or begin to disengage because they are bored or confused or feel stupid. Such acting up or avoidance may then be seen or responded to as a "behaviour problem" rather than a communication problem. As a result, the communication needs may go unseen and unmet. And unmet emotional needs are the roots of what can become lifelong mental health issues.'[27] I was conscious that some of the kids I worked with back then in my early days in Hobart were possibly now residents at Risdon.

Communication problems are becoming more clearly understood as factors that might lead to prison. It is well documented that there is a very high degree of illiteracy in prisons – statistics vary in international studies between 60 per cent and 90 per cent. Here in Australia, recorded figures show that around 50 per cent of children who end up in the youth justice system have severe language impairment. The figures for language-based impairment in adult prisons are not known, but it is obvious that when people turn eighteen and become adults, the problem doesn't go away.

In 2013, under the aegis of Chatter Matters, I contacted the Prisoner Education and Training Unit at Risdon Prison and offered my professional services pro bono to assist with the high level of illiteracy among prisoners. They welcomed the offer and I set up a pilot program I called Just Sentences.

The first client I worked with in Risdon Prison was in his fifties. His speech production was similar to many of the children I work with. He'd never had any treatment for it. He was a clever man, and his comprehension of spoken language was good, but he had never learned to read because of the complexities of the sound-processing that he struggled with, though he could identify about twenty words in print, including 'stop', 'car' and his name. He'd been trying to learn to read with a prison-based volunteer tutor for about twelve months but had not made progress.

The first thing I do with a new client is a phonological processing assessment, which determines which skills need to be developed in that client. This client, for instance, could not discriminate between individual speech sounds, such as P and B. Another classic example of his profile was illustrated by the word 'farm'. If I said to him, 'Say "farm" but don't say F,' he couldn't tell me what the word would be that was left over. Someone who can read could picture the words 'farm' and 'arm' in their mind, as well as hear the sounds of the word, but not my client. He didn't get pictures of words arriving in his mind, which is a skill that normally begins to appear as children learn to read. His issue was based on a phonological problem that can be addressed with training. So I set about teaching the discrimination and discernment of each of the individual speech sounds.

Within four months, my client was reading books at Grade 3 to 5 level and writing pages and pages of reflective dialogue. Having discovered that letters represent sounds and learning to discern what individual sounds were and that he could link them to letters, he brought the full force of his intelligence to the process. 'Is that what reading's about?' he exclaimed to me delightedly.

I see many similar breakthroughs with adult clients in a surprisingly short period of time. A good assessment at the beginning tells us what we need to do to get the most incisive activity happening to stimulate the skill that's missing. One grateful prisoner told me, 'You were able to figure out from my tests how I process sounds. You got inside my head and worked out what I couldn't do and showed me how to do it! You were the one who worked it out.'

Achieving literacy has a dramatic impact on the life of a person who struggles to communicate. It affects their relationship with themselves and with others. It is essential for most employment and for creating a meaningful life, while imparting such skills has a powerful ripple effect that extends well beyond the teacher and the student. It enlarges and enriches us all as individuals and as community. Withholding these skills diminishes us all.

I passionately believe that language and literacy are linked to human rights and equity. Article 19 of the Universal Declaration of Human Rights, for example, states that 'Everyone has the right to freedom of opinion and expression'. Speech pathologists are calling for communication to be recognised as a basic human right, as without the capacity to communicate, people cannot express themselves in order to exercise those rights.

The outstanding success of Just Sentences led me in 2014 to introduce Just Time, a program based on the work of Circle of Security International, creator of the parenting program Circle of Security Parent DVD Program®. Using the Circle of Security as its central tool, Just Time comprises an eight-week course using reflective dialogue within a space that is safe and trusted, and in which prisoners who have children can share their stories at a deep level, exploring how they parent and how they were parented.

As far as we know, this was the first time that this group-based parenting program had been used in prisons. Outcomes have been extraordinary. Participants quickly see the benefits of developing a loving, nurturing relationship with their children and also see benefits in all their relationships, including their relationship with themselves. Just Time is now being run on government funding in one women's prison and two men's prisons in Tasmania.

In 2015 and 2016, I did a criminology degree to bring myself a more scholarly understanding of what I was doing in the prison system. I was confident about my clinical work with individuals but realised I didn't know that much about this new context within which I was working. I felt the need to have a greater level of understanding. I also wanted to know that what I was doing I was doing well.

In 2019 Chatter Matters was renamed Connect42. This was to honour its origins in Tasmania, as the 42 degrees south line runs through the heart of the state. It also playfully riffed on Douglas Adam's *The Hitchhiker's Guide to the Galaxy*, where 42 was named 'the meaning of life, the universe, and everything' – we see connection as the meaning of life, the universe and everything, so Connect42! Also, we learned that 42 is the ASCII code for the asterisk, the wildcard with which anything might happen and all things are possible, including Connect 42's aim of 100 per cent literacy in Tasmania. In working towards this goal, I feel that my purpose is fully realised.

The scope of Connect42 has expanded to include not only prisoners but also people experiencing homelessness and other disadvantages, including living with a disability. Qualities above all others that I value in this work are kindness, love and courage – especially kindness. It is a quality that makes communication work more effectively. It truly connects people. Kindness emerges from courage, attention to others and the generous self-acceptance that grows from the hard work of looking within.

In his book *The Courage to Teach: Exploring the Inner Landscape of a Teacher's Life* (1997), Parker Palmer wrote: 'Good teaching cannot be reduced to technique; good teaching comes from the identity and integrity of the teacher.' I learned at an early age the damage inflicted when a teacher lacks kindness.

'I felt it was my duty to see that Chinese food was appreciated for its complexity, for its simplicity, its beauty, its health-giving properties – for all the things I loved about it.'

Elizabeth Chong

Sharing the joy of Chinese food

I know people love Chinese food, but I still don't think they really understand the depth and beauty of it. For us Chinese food is not just to satisfy hunger; it has a spiritual and symbolic aspect. There's a sense of connectedness. In the Chinese way, we put our chopsticks in the same plate as everyone else, we share the same soup, we look at each other and say, 'That was so good.' Chinese food adds another level of joy to life.

My family were pioneers in introducing Chinese food to Australia, starting with my grandfather, Chen Ah Kew, who came to Victoria in the 1850s. He was about seventeen. He worked as an indentured labourer, clearing the bush and making roads, opening up land for European pastoralists. He was known as Jimmy. He was sent to Wahgunyah, a small settlement on the banks of the Murray in north-western Victoria. He couldn't read or write in either Chinese or English but was an enterprising man, and before long he was sponsoring other Chinese workers, whom he also supervised. He looked after their interests. He opened the general store in Wahgunyah and imported goods for miners working on the goldfields. He was fifty-eight when he married my grandmother. It was an arranged marriage, as there were few Chinese women in Australia at the time. Grandmother was eighteen when she came to live in Wahgunyah with her husband. In 1901, when my father was five, they went back to China, as my grandfather wanted to bury his bones there.

My dad, William Wing Young, eventually returned to Australia with his three brothers, his sister and mother. He was sixteen. Chinese people put their surnames first and first names last, so in Australia our family name became Wing Young, not Chen. My father and his brothers set up a wholesale fruit business, Wing Young & Company, in Melbourne's Queen Victoria Market. It was very successful and became one of the largest in Victoria. Dad married Lee Jun Wei, a bride also chosen for him in China. They settled in Carlton, where my sister Ruby and brother Tom were born. When Mum was pregnant with her third child, Irene, the White Australia Policy came into force and she was told she had to leave the country even though her husband and children were Australian citizens.

Dad sold the house and took his family on a ship back to China, stopping at Hong Kong on the way, where Irene was born. Ironically this made Irene a British subject and free to live in Australia. I was born in Canton in 1931, where we lived with my grandmother while Dad commuted back and forth between China and Melbourne. It took five years to sort out the visa issues, and finally in 1934 we all came to Australia and moved into rooms above the family factory by the Queen Victoria Market.

Ladies from the local Church of Christ used to go to the market to convert the 'heathens'. Early Chinese migrant men regularly went to their free English language classes on Tuesdays and Thursdays, where the Bible was used as a textbook. The Sunday school teacher there gave us children English names, which is how I became Elizabeth and Bessie to my friends and family. My Chinese name is Yut Yi.

The family firm was flourishing, and Dad set up another business separate from his brothers, which he called Wing Lee & Company, Lee being my mother's maiden name. Like his father, Dad couldn't read or write but was a smart businessman. He provided Chinese food to the trade and quickly realised that Australians loved the tiny pork mince dumplings known as dim sims. Mum, along with other women, used to make them by hand but couldn't keep up with the demand.

Dad was very community-minded and concerned for the many elderly Chinese from the goldfield days who hadn't gone back home. He thought if he could manufacture dim sims on a large-enough scale, these men could make an income selling them. He heard of the machine-made sausage rolls sold in the Lyons Corner House tea shops in London and went to see for himself. On returning to Melbourne, he found a German engineer who made a similar machine for him, and he started churning dim sims out by the thousand. He sold them at wholesale prices to the old miners who went around with their caravans selling them at the races, at the football and to workers in the munitions factories.

One day, my brother Tom was taking a delivery of dim sims to an old miner based in Cheltenham. He stopped at Mordialloc to go fishing with his friend, Joe, who ran a fish-and-chip shop. When Tom gave him some dim sims to heat up for lunch, Joe had no idea what to do with them, so he deep-fried them. They were delicious. Joe told his friends, and in no time word spread and all the fish-and-chip shops in Melbourne started selling dim sims. It was crazy. Food writer Jill Dupleix tells me that Victorians today eat nine million dim sims a week. That's thanks to William Wing Young!

Like all migrants, my parents valued education and wanted the best for their six children: four girls and two boys. They asked people which were the best schools and sent me and my three sisters to Presbyterian Ladies College in East Melbourne and my two brothers to Scotch College. Dad's Chinese compatriots were surprised that he spent so much money on educating his daughters, but he insisted that girls were just as important as boys. One of my school friends, Deirdre Reid, invited me to her home for the night. I was fourteen and to my surprise Dad had no hesitation in saying yes. Generally Chinese parents liked to keep their children close, nervous they might be unduly influenced by western ways and forget about being Chinese. My father thought differently.

At Deirdre's was the first time I had a western meal. The table was beautifully laid out with a cloth and flowers and cutlery. I was amazed. A Chinese table is only set with the rice bowl and chopsticks. The food is the decoration. Deirdre's mother was a fine cook. She produced a rabbit casserole that evening – I've loved rabbit casserole ever since. And there were vegetables in big tureens and homemade bread, a cake, scones with jam and cream. It was all laid out on the table. I still remember how embarrassed I was as I didn't know how to eat English food or use a knife and fork. The Chinese way is never to eat more of one thing than another and to be aware of other people's needs. I helped myself to a little of everything, including the rabbit casserole and the cake and the scones with jam and cream, and put it all on my plate!

I dreamed of becoming a musician or a journalist but instead enrolled at the Victorian College of Education and became a trainee teacher at Balwyn State School. While I was there, the education department decreed that newly qualified teachers had to spend a year teaching in a rural school, but my parents felt that their daughter should not live away from home at the age of eighteen. Ironically, I met my future husband at that time and soon had romance and marriage in mind rather than teaching.

As a young wife – and I think even before I had my first child – my path to teaching others how to cook Chinese food was marked out for me. It started when my neighbours in North Balwyn asked me to show them how to cook rice and I found myself also giving them hints on how to cook more interesting meals and avoid their vegetables being so limp. The next thing I knew, I was being asked to give cooking demonstrations as a fundraiser for many local causes, such as fixing the roof of the local Anglican church. Soon I had a diary full of cooking demonstrations.

As the years went by, I had four lovely children, and in 1961 started to give cooking classes at my home for a group of local schoolteachers. I made many good friends but knew life was not what it should be. My husband and I were practically living separate lives and had very little in common. I was feeling very lonely and knew I had to make plans. It was clear to me that the crucial first step was financial independence. After four difficult years I made a decision and was able to put down a deposit on a small townhouse in Box Hill. By then two of my children had left home, my older son to get married and my younger daughter to work in New Zealand. I moved with my younger son and older daughter.

The next big step was setting up my cooking school. I found a large room above a beautiful pastry shop in Kooyong called Croutons Fine Foods. It's still there today. I painted the room, partitioned off an office, installed a bench with wok stations, bought a big refrigerator and thirty folding chairs, and I was in business. It wasn't anything like taking classes at home, which essentially was a hobby. The new cooking school was business. It was 1974 and mine was among the first Chinese cooking schools in Victoria.

TURNING POINTS

My life soon changed dramatically. The cooking school boomed even though my classes were never advertised. People came through word of mouth. I ran six-week courses, teaching up to ten large classes a week. They were all demonstration-style, with me cooking each dish and students sitting and watching and tasting. I had to do a lot of shopping for ingredients. There were only a couple of Chinese wholesalers around at the time which I used, and I bought all my fresh produce at the Queen Victoria Market. I wrote out all my recipes by hand and had to keep careful accounts. I often didn't get home till midnight. I worked very, very hard but loved teaching, and Chinese food became my passion.

After six years I was able to put a deposit on a lovely family home in Hawthorn and moved the cooking school there. One of my students, Claire Kearney, was the chief buyer at the Hill of Content bookshop in the city and she encouraged me to write a cookery book. Such an idea had never occurred to me, but I took her advice and started writing, putting everything I knew into the book. *The First Happiness: Chinese Cooking for Australia* was published in 1982 and proved to be a bestseller.

Another of my students worked for Channel Ten. She introduced me to one of the senior people there, who invited me to take part in their show, *Good Morning Melbourne*. I was really nervous until Annette Allison, the co-host, told me, 'Elizabeth, just be yourself.' I relaxed and really enjoyed it. I felt I was contributing to the appreciation of Chinese food. Chinese restauranteurs saw me as being one avenue through which they could reach a wider public. While people loved Chinese food, they saw it as being cheap and cheerful. I hated that. I felt it was my duty to see that Chinese food was appreciated for its complexity, for its simplicity, its beauty, its health-giving properties – for all the things I loved about it.

Some years later I was approached by Weldon Russell, well-known Sydney publishers. They were doing a series of coffee-table books on the heritage of cooking from different countries and wanted one on China. They had a team in Sydney to test my recipes and a picture researcher who matched the recipes with paintings and photographs from museums around the world, including in China, Hong Kong, New York and Taiwan. *The Heritage of Chinese Cooking* came out in 1993. It was my seventh book. I was absolutely blown away when I saw the first print. The book was very, very beautiful and I felt proud of it.

There was the usual round of publicity when *The Heritage of Chinese Cooking* was published, including an appearance with Bert Newton on Channel Ten's *Good Morning Australia*. *Good Morning Melbourne* had ended a couple of years before and by then I was quite comfortable on television. After my appearance on *Good Morning Australia*, the producer came up to me and said, 'Bert wants you to come on regularly – will you come back next week?' Bert later told me I was a natural on television. I was on *Good Morning Australia* once a week, sometimes twice, for the next twelve years, and occasionally travelled with the show.

Bert Newton was very supportive and encouraging and contributed a lot to the success of my career. I became a public person and found myself recognised all over the country. People would write in for my recipes; they would come up to me in the street and say how much they enjoyed the show, that they never missed my Tuesday slot. It's lovely when you go to a restaurant or the supermarket and someone stops and smiles. It's very humbling.

I have given a lot to the Chinese food industry and feel I have been a bridge for our two cultures. Chinese food is now a part of Australian cuisine. Words like *sung choi bao*, *dim sim* and *stirfry* are a familiar part of the language.

TURNING POINTS

I was genuinely surprised in 2019 when I was made a Member of the Order of Australia for my contribution to the hospitality sector and my promotion of Chinese culture. It was official recognition that through my work I had changed the perception of Asian food in Australia and brought about a better understanding between my two worlds. Food is such a common language; it speaks directly to the heart and to the stomach.

Contributors

Yuot Ajang Alaak is a refugee from South Sudan who came to Australia with his family in May 1995. A father of four, he works in the mining industry as a hydrogeologist (groundwater engineer) and is a proud South Sudanese Australian. Yuot's book, *Father of the Lost Boys: A Memoir* (2020), was shortlisted for the New South Wales Premier's Literary Awards, the Western Australia Premier's Book Awards and the City of Freemantle Hungerford Award. Yuot was nominated as a Local Hero in the 2022 Australian of the Year Awards.

In her autobiography, *A Cook's Life,* **Stephanie Alexander AO** describes the powerful influence of family meals in her childhood. They brought together her mother's adventurous cooking, her father's love of books, the company of family, and passionate conversations about politics. Gatherings round a table remain one of the joys in Stephanie's life. In 1965 Stephanie and her first husband, Monty, opened the restaurant Jamaica House in Carlton. In 1976 she and her second husband, Maurice, opened Stephanie's Restaurant in Fitzroy. It moved to Hawthorn in 1980, where it won numerous Australian and international awards. Stephanie's Kitchen Garden Foundation, established in 2001, exposes children to the adventure of cooking and eating food they have grown. Stephanie has inspired generations of home cooks and transformed the way we think about food.

CONTRIBUTORS

Anthony Bartl is a journalist, filmmaker, public speaker, primary-school teacher and C1 quadriplegic. Over time he learned to accept the limitations of his body and challenges himself as much as he can physically, intellectually, emotionally and spiritually. He is the first quadriplegic in Australia to gain a degree – in fact, he has two degrees. He has a state-of-the-art wheelchair that he manoeuvres with his chin. He operates his computer and mobile phone with a stick held in his mouth. The internet enables him to study, research, read and keep in touch with the world. His passions are writing and the Hawthorn Football Club, and his goal is to help others with a disability and to change public perceptions of disability.

Jack Charles (1943–2022) was an Aboriginal Elder, actor, musician, potter and activist. By chance in the late 1960s he encountered New Theatre Melbourne and discovered a love of acting. His professional career began with a role in *The Blood Knot* in 1970. In 1971 he co-founded Nindethana, Australia's first Indigenous theatre group. In 2008 he was the subject of Amiel Courtin-Wilson's documentary *Bastardy*. Jack received a Lifetime Achievement Award in Victoria's Green Room Awards in 2014, the first Indigenous recipient, and a Red Ochre Award in 2019. In 2016 he was named Senior Victorian Australian of the Year for his work as an Elder and actor. In 2019 he published his memoir, *Jack Charles: Born-Again Blakfella*, described by Paul Kelly as 'a hell of a yarn, a celebration and a gift to us all, told by a huge-hearted, gutsy survivor'.

Elizabeth Chong AM is a celebrated chef, teacher of Chinese cooking and culture, television personality and writer of cookery books. She has been a major influence in introducing Chinese cuisine to Australia.

CONTRIBUTORS

Dishes she taught at her famous Chinese cooking school in Melbourne were an exotic novelty in the 1970s; they have since become standard fare for many Australians. In 1993, Elizabeth was inducted into the Melbourne Food and Wine Festival Legends Hall of Fame. Her seventh book, *The Heritage of Chinese Cooking*, was awarded the prestigious Prix La Mazille for International Cookbook of the Year in 1994 – she was the first non-French winner. The proudest moment of her career was being made a Member of the Order of Australia in 2019 for her service to the hospitality sector.

Inala Cooper is the director of Murrup Barak, the Melbourne Institute for Indigenous Development at the University of Melbourne. She is a Yawuru woman from Broome in the Kimberley, Western Australia, and grew up in southwest Victoria on Gunditjmara land. She also has Irish and German heritage. The daughter of barrister and human rights activist Mick Dodson and the niece of Senator Pat Dodson, Inala learned about social justice from an early age. She has a Master of Human Rights Law and serves on the boards of State Library Victoria, Jesuit Social Services, Culture Is Life and the Adam Briggs Foundation. Her book, *Marrul: Aboriginal Identity and the Fight for Rights*, was published in 2022.

Richard Cornish is a versatile and entertaining food writer, author, event host and professional photographer. He is a senior features writer for the Good Food section of *The Sydney Morning Herald* and *The Age* and author of the popular 'Brain Food' column. He has also written several books with MoVida chef Frank Camorra, including *MoVida Rustica: Spanish Traditions and Recipes* (2009) and *MoVida's Guide to Barcelona* (2011). Richard has been a commentator on the

CONTRIBUTORS

Seven Network series *Iron Chef Australia* and co-creative director of the Melbourne Food and Wine Festival. In 2019 he was inducted into the Melbourne Food and Wine Festival Legends Hall of Fame for his exceptional record in telling stories about Victorian food and drink.

In 1977, **Robyn Davidson** walked 2735 kilometres from Alice Springs to the coast of Western Australia. It was a journey that changed her life. *Tracks*, the book she published about the experience in 1980, inspired millions and launched Robyn on a career of travelling and writing. *Tracks* won the 1980 Thomas Cook Travel Book Award and became a film in 2013, starring Mia Wasikowska and Adam Driver and screening at the Venice Film Festival. Her journey across the desert opened up new worlds for Robyn: the world of nature, the world of writing, the world of Aboriginal peoples, the world of inner discovery. She has since published the books *Travelling Light* (1989), *Ancestors* (1989), *Desert Places* (1996) and the extended essay *No Fixed Address: Nomads and the Fate of the Planet* (2006).

Peter Doherty AC FRS FMedSci is an immunologist who, with his colleague Rolf Zinkernagel in the early 1970s, discovered how the immune system recognises virus-infected cells. In 1986, they were jointly awarded the Nobel Prize in Physiology or Medicine for their work. Professor Doherty was appointed Australian of the Year in 1997 and named Companion of the Order of Australia for his contribution to medicine and science. He was also named a National Living Treasure. In 2014, the University of Melbourne and the Royal Melbourne Hospital established the Peter Doherty Institute for Infection and Immunity. It is a world-renowned centre of excellence. Peter Doherty

CONTRIBUTORS

has written a number of books, including *An Insider's Plague Year*, published in August 2021 amid the Covid-19 crisis.

Gabrielle 'Didi' Dowling AM was sent to Mongolia by Ānanda Mārga in 1993 to teach yoga and meditation. On discovering the shocking condition and vulnerability of many young people, especially teenage girls who were living on the streets, she founded the Lotus Children's Centre in 1995. The organisation cares for abandoned children from a few weeks of age until they can reach independence, hopefully in their late teens and early twenties. In 2009, Didi was appointed a Member of the Order of Australia 'for service to the welfare of children in Mongolia as the founder and director of the Lotus Children's Centre and through programs to improve child health and educational development'.

From 1995 until 2003, **Allan Fels AO** was inaugural chairman of the Australian Competition and Consumer Commission (ACCC), a Labor initiative based on a merger of the Trade Practices Commission and the Prices Surveillance Authority. In 2002, the *Australian Financial Review* voted him the third most powerful man in the country, behind prime minister John Howard and treasurer Peter Costello. He became active in mental health advocacy after his daughter was diagnosed with schizophrenia. Fels chaired the National Mental Health Commission from 2012 to 2018, is patron of the Mental Health Council of Australia and was a commissioner for the Royal Commission into Mental Health in Victoria. He also chairs the Haven Foundation and serves on the board of SANE Australia. Fels, who has taught extensively at Monash University, is an adjunct professor at Monash University in

CONTRIBUTORS

the Faculty of Business and Economics and a professorial fellow at the University of Melbourne.

Anna Funder worked for the Australian government as a lawyer in human rights law, constitutional law and treaty negotiation before becoming a full-time writer in the late 1990s. Her first book, *Stasiland*, was published in 2003, and her second, *All That I Am*, in 2012. Among the many literary awards both books received, *Stasiland* won the UK's most prestigious award for nonfiction, the Samuel Johnson Prize, in 2004 and *All That I Am* won the Miles Franklin Prize in 2012. In 2009 Anna published *Courage, Survival, Greed* with Melissa Lucashenko and Christopher Kremmer, and in 2015 *The Girl with the Dogs*, a homage to Anton Chekhov's 'The Lady with the Dog'. Her feature, *Secret History*, about the files from Nazi death camps held in obscurity by German authorities, won the Maunder Prize for Journalism. Anna's upcoming work is the genre-bending *Wifedom: Mrs Orwell's Invisible Life* (2023).

Meliesa Judge owns and runs Liquid Metal Studios in Adelaide with her husband, Will Kuiper. The two work separately and together creating bronze sculptures, and are recognised internationally as being among the foremost producers of contemporary figurative sculptures in Australia. Meliesa's work is represented in private collections across Australia, Europe and the United States. She was granted a Churchill Fellowship in 2001.

Elena Kats-Chernin AO is one of Australia's finest, most prolific and widely celebrated composers. In a career spanning more than four decades, she has received numerous commissions from internationally renowned ensembles and symphony orchestras, opera houses, musical

CONTRIBUTORS

theatres, ballets, silent film companies and even private individuals. Her music incorporates a wide range of influences, including cabaret, tango, ragtime and klezmer, underpinned by a profound knowledge of classical music and modern European movements. Her first piece to attract worldwide acclaim was *Deep Sea Dreaming*, for the opening ceremony of the 2000 Olympic Games in Sydney, a collaboration with choreographer Meryl Tankard AO for the children's choir and orchestra. She was named an Officer of the Order of Australia in 2019 'for distinguished service to the performing arts, particularly to music, as an orchestral, operatic and chamber music composer'.

Margaret Leggatt AM advocated strongly for the development of community mental health services that would profoundly change the treatment and care of those suffering from schizophrenia when she established the Schizophrenia Fellowship of Victoria in 1978 and SANE Australia in 1986. She realised that families struggling to cope with a mentally ill child were wrongly blamed for causing it. Revolutionising support for them, she exposed inadequacies in the mental health system which continue to this day. Margaret was founding director of the Schizophrenia Fellowship for seventeen years, the last three of which she was also founding director of SANE Australia. She continued as director of SANE until 1987, when she was made a Member of the Order of Australia 'for services for those with schizophrenia and to their families'. In 2019 Margaret was called to give evidence at the Royal Commission into Mental Health Victoria. Her book co-written with poet Sandy Jeffs, *Out of the Madhouse* (2020), won the Oral History Award in the Victorian Community History Awards and was shortlisted for the 2021 Oral History Australia Awards.

CONTRIBUTORS

The Australian census in 2016 showed that of the 219,355 Vietnamese refugees who settled in Australia in the 1970s and 1980s, about half came by boat. Among them were Trung Luong and Huong Tran. They met and married in South Australia, and they placed a high value on the education of their five children. **Gia-Yen Luong** was the oldest and the only girl. She topped the class at her state high school in Adelaide and studied law at the University of New South Wales. In her fourth year at UNSW, she shocked her peers by deciding to become a teacher. In 2018 she received a Rhodes Scholarship, which she completed in 2019–20.

Rosalie Martin is a speech pathologist and criminologist with her own private practice in Hobart, specialising in services for children with autism spectrum disorder and language–literacy disorders. In 2012 she founded Chatter Matters Tasmania (since renamed Connect42), a charity building awareness and skills in communication which aims to transform language literacy and learning for all Tasmanians. The following year, she set up a pilot program, Just Sentences, in Hobart's Risdon Prison to assist with high levels of illiteracy among prisoners. The inability to read, she knows, put people at a serious disadvantage, impairing their ability to connect and communicate with others. In 2017 she was named Tasmanian Australian of the Year for her extraordinary work with prisoners. The impact of her work continues to be profound.

In her memoir, **Fiona Patten MP** describes the making of one of Australia's most effective politicians with candour, humour and wry self-knowledge, calling herself a 'libertarian ingénue'. Add the words 'socially progressive warrior' and you capture something of the scope of Fiona's impact as an HIV/AIDS educator and activist. She was

CONTRIBUTORS

CEO of the Eros Association, Australia's national adult industry lobby group, before being elected to the Victorian Legislative Council in 2014 representing the Sex Party, which she founded in 2009. In 2017, the Sex Party became the Reason Party. In July 2020, Fiona Patten was named Humanist of the Year, a prestigious honour awarded by the Council of Australian Humanist Societies in recognition of someone who 'does great things for the public good'.

Henry Reynolds' remarkable contribution in penetrating the Great Australian Silence about Australia's Indigenous peoples came out of the ugly racism he encountered in Queensland in the 1960s. Through years of meticulous research, he exposed the violence behind the 'heroic' view of European settlement in Australia, sparking the so-called history wars. His detractors spoke of his 'black armband' version of Australian history; his response was 'better a black armband than a white blindfold'. He has received numerous awards for his books and essays, including the Ernest Scott Prize for History (1982), the Banjo Award for Nonfiction (1996), Queensland Premier's Literary Awards (2000 and 2008) and the Prime Minister's Literary Award (2009, with Marilyn Lake). He is a fellow of the Academy of the Social Sciences in Australia and the Australian Academy of the Humanities.

Jane Rowe OAM is the founding CEO of the Mirabel Foundation, the only organisation in Australia specifically addressing the needs of children who have been orphaned or abandoned due to parental drug use. Mirabel has now been running for more than twenty years and includes notable ambassadors Jimmy Barnes, Dr Patch Adams, Rebecca Barnard and Deborah Conway. The foundation provides support to families in crisis, individual and group counselling, after-school care

CONTRIBUTORS

and a range of life-changing programs and activities. Mirabel was recognised as an example of best practice by the Australian National Council on Drugs. Jane has received several awards for her work, including the Victorian Local Hero Australian of the Year Award in 2015.

In his poem *An Absolutely Ordinary Rainbow*, Les Murray writes about the solitary dignity of a man standing alone in Martin Place, Sydney, weeping: '... the man no one approaches / simply weeps, and does not cover it.' Murray could have been describing **Peter Sharp**, who in mid-2010 stood in Sydney's Macquarie Shopping Centre and wept. After the denial of his insurance claim for disability, Peter found a professional purpose in his childhood passion for animal photography. Since setting up Tame & Wild Studio in 2017, he has won numerous national and international awards for his work, including the Australian Institute of Professional Photography New South Wales Pet/Animal Photographer of the Year in 2018 and an honourable mention in the 2020 prestigious International Photography Lucie Awards in Carnegie Hall, New York. His book is *Lost But Found* (2019).

Julie Sprigg received an unexpected invitation to Ethiopia in 2004, where she worked initially at clinics run by Catholic nuns and then taught Ethiopia's first physiotherapists at the University of Gondar Hospital. She describes her experience in *Small Steps: A Physio in Ethiopia* (2020), which was shortlisted for the 2018 City of Fremantle Hungerford Award for an unpublished manuscript. On her return to Australia, Julie took up a position with CBM, an international organisation aiming to break the cycle of poverty and disability, running programs for people with disabilities in developing countries.

CONTRIBUTORS

She then worked with Save the Children Australia as a program quality adviser, focused on the inclusion of children with disabilities in their mainstream programs. She now has a position with the state government in Western Australia, evaluating government programs to overcome social disadvantage.

At a masterclass at the Deutsche Oper Berlin in 2014, legendary German mezzo-soprano Christa Ludwig described **Siobhan Stagg**'s voice as 'one of the most beautiful I've ever heard'. What greater tribute could one of the world's finest opera singers coming to the end of her career pay to a young singer at the beginning of hers? Siobhan has won great acclaim for performances around the world and has a very clear take on the value of her art. She sees opera as 'providing a service that enables people to disconnect from the stresses and troubles of everyday life and connect to a moment of beauty'. She is inspired by the words of Danish director Kasper Holten, who sees opera as 'the emotion fitness centre for life'. What else in our lives, she points out, gives us the opportunity to spend three hours thinking about love, hate and the broader range of human emotions in an artistic setting?

Gillian Triggs is working in Geneva as Assistant High Commissioner for International Protection to the United National High Commissioner for Refugees. It is an appointment that crowns an extraordinary legal career spanning more than fifty years. When she accepted the position in 2019, the High Commissioner, Filippo Grandi, said of her: 'Gillian Triggs brings to UNHCR extensive expertise, knowledge and vast experience in international refugee protection that will contribute enormously to our efforts to protect, assist and find solutions for those forced by violence and persecution to flee their homes.' The president of

CONTRIBUTORS

the Australian Human Rights Commission between 2012 and 2017, Gillian is the recipient of numerous awards, including Humanist of the Year (2018) and the prestigious Ruth Bader Ginsburg Medal of Honor (2021), which is bestowed upon distinguished female jurists and leaders from around the world.

Andrew Wilkie is the Independent federal member for Clark in Tasmania, a position he has held since 2010. He served as an officer in the Australian Army, from where he was seconded to the Office of National Assessments as an intelligence analyst. His time there came to a dramatic end when he resigned from ONA in protest over the Australian government's involvement in the Iraq War. As an independent member of parliament, Andrew has the freedom to continue to speak out on what he calls 'tough issues'. These have included gambling, the detention of asylum seekers, climate change, the illegal bugging of the Timor-Leste cabinet and the harassment and prosecution of whistleblower Witness K and his lawyer, Bernard Collaery. His is one of the loudest voices in the Australian parliament condemning the unjust treatment of whistleblower Julian Assange.

Acknowledgements

All the people who agreed to be included in this book did so with great generosity and trust. Hearing their stories was a privilege. It was also an enriching experience both for me, the listener, and hopefully for them, the storytellers. I thank them all. I believe their stories will also enrich the hearts and minds of those who read them.

I thank Brenda Niall for her belief in this book, and for her gift of the foreword and offering to launch it into the world. Her words capture what I hoped to achieve. Three more than generous friends, Jill Fenwick, Penelope Hughes and Helen Sykes, accompanied me on the journey of this book. From the beginning they read every interview and gave valuable feedback and encouragement. Tiffany Blackman transcribed all but one of the interviews in partnership with her father, John Blackman. They did a great job. My thanks as well to Annie Chapman for regularly rescuing me from technical crises. I am also grateful to Anthony Baird, Mary O'Brien, Megan Evans and Rodford Belcher, who helped shape my initial concept, and to Noah Mankowitz for his wisdom.

I was thrilled when my long-time friend, publishing consultant Robert Sessions, accepted me as a client and thank him for his efforts on my behalf and for his encouragement and commitment. Rob introduced me to Julia Carlomagno, director and publisher of Monash University Publishing. She and her wonderful team, Joanne Mullins, Sarah Cannon, Les Thomas and Sam van der Plank, have been remarkable.

ACKNOWLEDGEMENTS

Being accepted by them was a turning point in the life of this book. I had no idea when we first started to work together how complex the process would be. Julia has been meticulous in her editing and her guidance with the text. Les Thomas came up with the powerful cover design that proved to be a metaphor for the path we followed. Jo has done an amazing job meeting the challenge of dealing with twenty-five photos from twenty-five sources and bringing together the pages. Sarah is encouragingly confident in her marketing and Sam is ever-helpful with the inevitable paperwork. Together, they ensured that the book looks and feels and reads well. They have been a joy to work with.

Australia's Western Desert people have a word, *Kanyirninpa*, that combines physical, emotional and spiritual sustaining, loving and nurturing. The closest equivalent in English is 'holding'. I have experienced *Kanyirninpa* in many, many ways while working on this project. From the start I have been 'held' by the love and kindness of my family and friends. I thank each and every one.

Image Credits

Yuot Alaak by Manuel Goria © Manolomedia; Stephanie Alexander by Armelle Habib © Stephanie Alexander; Anthony Bartl © Reef Magic Cruises; Jack Charles © Chris Riordan, with permission from Patrice Capogreco on behalf of the family; Elizabeth Chong © Elizabeth Chong; Inala Cooper © Inala Cooper; Richard Cornish © Sunday Cornish-Treloar; Robyn Davidson by Julie Millowick © Julie Millowick and Robyn Davidson; Peter Doherty © Doherty Institute; Gabrielle 'Didi' Dowling © Lotus Children's Centre; Elena Kats-Chernin by Vicki Lauren © Elena Kats-Chernin; Allan Fels © Allan Fels collection; Anna Funder © Anna Funder collection; Margaret Leggatt © Nico Clark; Gia-Yen Luong © Stewart Francis; Rosalie Martin © Paul Barrington; Meliesa Judge © Will Kuiper; Fiona Patten © Fiona Patten collection; Henry Reynolds by Mark Horstman © Henry Reynolds; Jane Rowe © James Rowe; Peter Sharp © photographer unknown, Peter Sharp collection; Julie Sprigg © Leigh Miller; Siobhan Stagg © Simon Pauly; Gillian Triggs by Susan Hopper © UNHCR / Susan Hopper; Andrew Wilkie © David Foote of AUSPIC; Mary Ryllis Clark © Dina Kapaklis.

Notes

1   Reed, Richard, *If I Could Tell You Just One Thing …*, Canongate, Edinburgh, 2016.

2   The success of the pastoral industry in Queensland and the Northern Territory depended on cheap Aboriginal labour. Payment often comprised tobacco, clothing, tea and sugar. The Conciliation and Arbitration Commission ruling on equal wages came into force in 1968. Few Aboriginal people were paid award rates and whole communities were driven off land they had lived on for generations. They mostly drifted to the cities, where they were forced to live off 'sit-down money' (unemployment benefits).

3   Russel Ward's *The Australian Legend* (1965) presented a vision of the bush as egalitarian. In the blurb for his lecture 'Rethinking *The Australian Legend*', Sir John Monash Distinguished Professor of History Graeme Davison noted, 'In tracing Australia's national ethos to the folksongs and ballads of the "nomad tribe" of bush workers, Ward and his Leftist contemporaries were rejecting the high culture of international modernism and reviving an older, romantic paradigm of national origins.'

4   The Holt government held a referendum on 27 May 1967 in which the people of Australia voted overwhelmingly to amend the Constitution to include Aboriginal peoples as part of the population and allow the Commonwealth to create laws for them.

5   Kurt Posel was a German immigrant who taught Robyn how to handle camels. When Posel's aggressive manner drove her away, Robyn continued her training with local Afghan camel trainer, Sallay Mahomet.

6   The footage is available to view at www.youtube.com/watch?v=fuSsfLzqmxA and www.youtube.com/watch?v=RYOoQop92rI. In introducing Anthony to the audience, host Eddie McGuire noted that he was 'the first Aussie with C1 quadriplegia to complete a degree' – a remarkable achievement.

7   To watch the hour-long documentary, *Unwheel Adventures*, contact Anthony via email at bartlmania@gmail.com for the link and password. Anthony is also on Facebook.

8   Craig Duby was convicted of two offences of driving under the influence in 1989 and 1990, hence the moniker.

9   In August 2020, for example, when the Andrews Labor government wanted to extend the State of Emergency in Victoria by twelve months, Fiona Patten led the move in parliament to a compromise of six months.

NOTES

10   Built in 1871 as the Kew Asylum, the institution was eventually renamed Willsmere when it became a mental hospital in the 1960s. It closed in December 1988 and the site was redeveloped as residential properties.

11   A ger is a round, portable tent made of timber and covered with skins or felt. Gers are designed to be readily dismantled and moved. Rebuilding takes about two hours. They have been used by nomads in the Mongolian steppes for more than 1000 years.

12   The Marumali Program was developed for members of the Stolen Generation by Aunty Lorraine Peeters to heal the social and emotional damage this inflicted.

13   Established in Fitzroy in 1994 and now located in Richmond, Turning Point Alcohol and Drug Centre provides clinical treatment and support for people with substance addiction, as well as clinical and epidemiological research and development.

14   A Kadaitcha man is an Australian Aboriginal medicine man.

15   The Archie Roach Foundation was founded in 2014 to nurture meaningful and potentially life-changing opportunities for First Nations artists.

16   Smiling Minds is Australia's leading mindfulness provider, aiming to provide life-long tools to support healthy minds. NAIDOC stands for National Aborigines and Islanders Day Observance Committee.

17   On 26 August 2020, a two-and-a-half-year-old was released after spending her entire life in detention. There are now no asylum-seeker children in overseas detention.

18   On 4 June 2019 the Australian Federal Police (AFP) raided the home of News Corp journalist Annika Smethurst after she published a top-secret government plan to give Australian cyber spies unprecedented powers. The following day, 5 June, the AFP raided the Sydney offices of the ABC in relation to a *Four Corners* program that revealed how Australian special forces in Afghanistan allegedly killed civilians and covered it up.

19   Australian journalist Wilfred Burchett was the first 'western' reporter to file from Hiroshima after the dropping of the atomic bomb. A staunch communist, he also reported on the Korean and Vietnam wars and often presented another side to the conflict.

20   Quoted in Alain de Botton, *Religion for Atheists: A Non-Believer's Guide to the Uses of Religion*, Penguin Books, London, 2012, p. 233.

21   The book is *When the Children Arrive: A Resource Book for Kinship Carers by the Mirabel Foundation*, 2020, available at www.mirabelfoundation.org.au/events-campaigns/mirabel-resource-books. It is now in its fourth edition, after being published in 2001 and updated in 2003 and 2004.

22   Formed in Frankfurt in 1980, the Ensemble Modern is an international ensemble dedicated to performing the music of modern composers. They developed a close collaboration with Elena.

23   The Melba Opera Trust was formed in 2008 to fill the gap created by the closure of the Melba Memorial Conservatorium of Music, where Dame Nellie taught until her

NOTES

death in 1931. It manages her bequest to honour her final wish for a scholarship for young Australian opera singers 'so that another Melba may arise'.

24   In 2020 Siobhan was the first alumna to be appointed a director of the board of the Melba Opera Trust.

25   Teach for Australia is a not-for-profit, federally funded organisation that attracts an outstanding cohort of graduate applicants, who go through a demanding, multi-stage selection process.

26   Lake Condah, also known by its Gunditjmara name Tae Rak, is on the edge of the Budj Bim National Park but within the Budj Bim Cultural Landscape. It became part of the National Heritage List in 2004 and was added to UNESCO's World Heritage List in 2019.

27   Quoted in *The Hobart Mercury*, 17 August 2018. Now available on the Connect42 website.

About the Editor

Mary Ryllis Clark is a writer and historian. The author of several books, she also wrote a fortnightly column for *The Age*, 'Historic Victoria', from 1992 to 2005. Mary migrated from London to Australia in 1974, lives in a historic factory in the Melbourne suburb of Fitzroy and enjoys her city's rich and diverse cultural life. Her most recent book is *A Tear in the Glass* (Anchor Books, 2018), a biography of the Australian director and curator Nina Stanton.

Ingram Content Group UK Ltd.
Milton Keynes UK
UKHW042019120323
418425UK00003B/36